Fodor's InFocus

D0453723

GRAND CANYON NATIONAL PARK

1st Edition

Where to Stay and Eat
for All Budgets

Must-See Sights
and Local Secrets

Ratings You Can Trust

Fodor's Travel Publications New York, Toronto, London, Sydney, Auckland
www.fodors.com

FODOR'S IN FOCUS GRAND CANYON NATIONAL PARK

Series Editor: Douglas Stallings

Editor: Amy B Wang

Editorial Production: Astrid deRidder

Editorial Contributors: Cara LaBrie, Carrie Miner, Neil Munshi

Maps & Illustrations: David Lindroth and Mark Stroud, *cartographers*; Bob Blake and Rebecca Baer, *map editors*

Design: Fabrizio LaRocca, *creative director*; Guido Caroti, *art director*; Ann McBride, *designer*; Melanie Marin, *senior picture editor*

Cover Photo (hikers overlook the River Nankoweap): Kerrick James

Production/Manufacturing: Matthew Struble

SPECIAL SALES

This book is available for special discounts for bulk purchases for sales promotions or premiums. Special editions, including personalized covers, excerpts of existing books, and corporate imprints, can be created in large quantities for special needs. For more information, write to Special Markets/Premium Sales, 1745 Broadway, MD 6-2, New York, NY 10019, or e-mail specialmarkets@randomhouse.com.

AN IMPORTANT TIP & AN INVITATION

Although all prices, opening times, and other details in this book are based on information supplied to us at press time, changes occur all the time in the travel world, and Fodor's cannot accept responsibility for facts that become outdated or for inadvertent errors or omissions. **So always confirm information when it matters,** especially if you're making a detour to visit a specific place. Your experiences—positive and negative—matter to us. If we have missed or misstated something, **please write to us.** We follow up on all suggestions. Contact the In Focus Grand Canyon National Park editor at editors@fodors.com or c/o Fodor's at 1745 Broadway, New York, NY 10019.

PRINTED IN THE UNITED STATES OF AMERICA

10 9 8 7 6 5 4 3 2 1

Be a Fodor's Correspondent

Your opinion matters. It matters to us. It matters to your fellow Fodor's travelers, too. And we'd like to hear it. In fact, we *need* to hear it. When you share your experiences and opinions, you become an active member of the Fodor's community. Here's how you can help improve Fodor's for all of us.

Tell us when we're right. We rely on local writers to give you an insider's perspective. But our writers and staff editors also depend on you. Your positive feedback is a vote to renew our recommendations for the next edition.

Tell us when we're wrong. We update most of our guides every year. But things change. If any of our descriptions are inaccurate or inadequate, we'll incorporate your changes in the next edition and will correct factual errors at fodors.com *immediately*.

Tell us what to include. You probably have had fantastic travel experiences that aren't yet in Fodor's. Why not share them with a community of like-minded travelers? Share your discoveries and experiences with everyone directly at fodors.com. Your input may lead us to add a new listing or a higher recommendation.

Give us your opinion instantly at our feedback center at www.fodors.com/feedback. You may also e-mail editors@fodors.com with the subject line "Grand Canyon National Park Editor." Or send your nominations, comments, and complaints by mail to Grand Canyon National Park Editor, Fodor's, 1745 Broadway, New York, NY 10019.

Happy Traveling!

Tim Jarrell, Publisher

CONTENTS

ABOUT THIS BOOK

Our Ratings

We wouldn't recommend a place that wasn't worth your time, but sometimes a place is so experiential that superlatives don't do it justice: you just have to be there to know. These sights, properties, and experiences get our highest rating, **Fodor's Choice**, indicated by orange stars throughout this book. Black stars highlight sights and properties we deem **Highly Recommended**, places that our writers, editors, and readers praise again and again for consistency and excellence.

Credit Cards

Want to pay with plastic? **AE, D, DC, MC, V** after restaurant and hotel listings indicate whether American Express, Discover, Diners Club, MasterCard, and Visa are accepted.

Restaurants

Unless we state otherwise, restaurants are open for lunch and dinner daily. We mention dress only when there's a specific requirement and reservations only when they're essential or not accepted—it's always best to book ahead.

Hotels

Unless we tell you otherwise, you can assume that the hotels have private bath, phone, TV, and air-conditioning. We always list facilities but not whether you'll be charged an extra fee to use them, so when pricing accommodations, find out what's included.

Many Listings
- ★ Fodor's Choice
- ★ Highly recommended
- ⊠ Physical address
- ⊹ Directions
- ⌖ Mailing address
- ☎ Telephone
- 🖷 Fax
- ⊕ On the Web
- ✍ E-mail
- 🎫 Admission fee
- ☉ Open/closed times
- Ⓜ Metro stations
- ⊟ Credit cards

Hotels & Restaurants
- 🏨 Hotel
- ↔ Number of rooms
- ⌂ Facilities
- ⦵ Meal plans
- ✕ Restaurant
- ⌕ Reservations
- ⌀ Smoking
- 🍺 BYOB
- ✕🏨 Hotel with restaurant that warrants a visit

Outdoors
- ⛳ Golf
- ⛺ Camping

Other
- ⌚ Family-friendly
- ⇨ See also
- ⊠ Branch address
- ☞ Take note

PLANNER

Top Reasons to Go

The Grand Canyon is one of the great natural wonders in the contiguous United States—and a UNESCO World Heritage Site. It's one place about which you really want to say, "Been there, done that!"

Painted desert, sandstone canyon walls, pine and fir forests, mesas, plateaus, volcanic features, the Colorado River, streams, and waterfalls make for some jaw-dropping moments.

Outdoor junkies can bike, boat, camp, fish, hike, ride mules, white-water raft, watch birds and wildlife, cross-country ski, and snowshoe.

Adults and kids can get schooled, thanks to free park-sponsored nature walks and interpretive programs.

Visitors can experience the canyon by air, land or water.

Getting There

When driving, the best access to the park from the east or south is from Flagstaff. Take U.S. 180 northwest 81 mi to the park's southern entrance and Grand Canyon Village. Or, for a scenic route with stopping points along the canyon rim, drive north from Flagstaff on U.S. 89, turn left at the junction of AZ 64 in Cameron (52 mi north of Flagstaff), and proceed north and west for an additional 57 mi until you reach Grand Canyon Village on the South Rim.

To go on to the North Rim, proceed north from Flagstaff on U.S. 89 to Bitter Springs. Then take U.S. 89A to the junction of Highway 67 and travel south on the highway for about 40 mi. From the west on Interstate 40, the most direct route to the South Rim is on U.S. 180 and Highway 64.

If you are driving to Grand Canyon West from Kingman, take Stockton Hill Road exit off Interstate 40. Head north 42 mi to Pierce Ferry Road. Travel north for 7 mi to Diamond Bar Road and turn east. In 21 mi, Diamond Bar Road comes to a dead end at Grand Canyon West Airport.

Hualapai headquarters are at Peach Springs, 80 mi west of Williams and 52 mi east of Kingman on historic Route 66. To reach the access point for the Havasu Trail leading down to Supai, travel 6 mi west of Peach Springs on Route 66, turn left on Indian Highway 18, and travel 68 mi to the dead end at Hualapai Hilltop. Be advised that there are no services on Indian Highway 18.

Getting Oriented

North Rim. Of the nearly 5 million people who visit the park annually, only 10% come here, but many believe the North Rim is even more gorgeous—and worth the extra effort. Accessible only from mid-May to mid-October (or the first good snowfall), the North Rim offers more solitude and even better views. Rather than staring into the canyon's depths, you get a true sense of its expanse.

South Rim. This is where the action is: Grand Canyon Village's lodging, camping, eateries, stores, and museums, plus plenty of trailheads into the canyon. Plus, it's open year-round. Shuttle routes, all free, cover 30-some stops, and visitors who'd rather relax than rough it can treat themselves to comfy hotel rooms and elegant restaurant meals.

West Rim. Though technically not part of the national park, the West Rim has some spectacular scenery and some of the most gorgeous waterfalls in the United States. The recently opened Skywalk is a U-shaped glass bridge suspended above the Colorado River—not for the faint of heart.

What It Costs In US$

¢	$	$$	$$$	$$$$
RESTAURANTS				
under $8	$8–$12	$13–$20	$21–$30	over $30
HOTELS				
under $70	$70–$120	$121–$175	$176–$250	over $250

Restaurant prices are per person for a main course at dinner and do not include any service charges or taxes. Hotel prices are for a double room in high season and do not include taxes, service charges, or resort fees.

Getting Around

There are three free shuttle routes in the park. Hermits Rest Route operates March through November between Grand Canyon Village and Hermits Rest. The Village Route operates year-round and provides the easiest access to the Canyon View Information Center. The Kaibab Trail Route travels from Canyon View Information Center to Yaki Point, including a stop at the South Kaibab Trailhead. In summer, South Rim roads are congested, and it's often easier (and sometimes required) to park your car and take the free shuttle. Running from 1 hour before sunrise until 1 hour after sunset, the shuttles arrive every 15 to 30 minutes. The roughly 30 stops are clearly marked throughout the park.

Shuttles take visitors to West Rim views at Eagle Point and Guano Point and the western town at Hualapai Ranch.

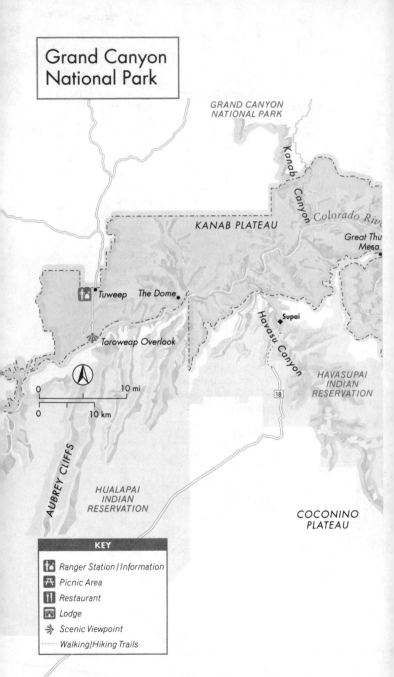

WHEN TO GO

There's not a bad time to visit the canyon, though summer and spring-break season are the busiest. Spring heralds colorful blankets of wildflowers. In summer, afternoon thunderstorms paint the canyon walls, darkening the colorful strata. Autumn color on the canyon oaks and snow-capped stone create images of change and peace in the fall and winter months. Since the North Rim gets considerable snowfall, the highways and facilities are closed from mid-October until mid-May. The South Rim, open year-round, is an exposed high-desert region, where the weather changes on a whim. Thanksgiving, Christmas, and New Year's can also get quite busy. If you visit from October through April, you'll likely experience light to moderate traffic and have no problem with parking.

Climate

The Grand Canyon covers 1,900 square mi on the Colorado Plateau; elevations range from 1,200 to 9,100 feet, which means climatic conditions vary immensely. Rainfall, for example, is more than 25 inches annually at the North Rim, whereas the South Rim collects but 16 inches in a typical year. The North Rim accumulates considerably more snow—about 130 inches per year—compared to less than half of that at the South Rim. (March is the month with the best chance for snow at the South Rim.) Temperatures vary widely, too. In summer, the canyon floor may easily reach 115°F. At the South Rim temperatures rarely exceed 90°F. It's seldom more than 80°F at the North Rim.

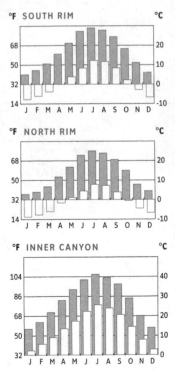

Welcome to the Grand Canyon

WORD OF MOUTH

"This was our 4th time to the Grand Canyon in 4 years, and it never ceases to amaze us with its beauty and grandeur."

—Gilbert56

By Carrie
Miner

THE GRAND CANYON is far more than an experience, it's an emotion—ask anyone who's visited, hiked, worked, or lived here. Many think it deserves a greater superlative than just "Grand" and, although it's easy to list the geological and historical statistics of the canyon, all of that becomes immaterial as you lose your breath when standing at the edge, whether for the first sunrise or the thousandth sunset.

In every way—biologically, historically, recreationally— Grand Canyon National Park is a superstar. One of the world's best examples of arid-land erosion, the canyon provides a record of three of the four eras of geological time. In addition to its diverse fossil record, the park reveals prehistoric traces of human adaptation to an unforgiving environment. It's also home to several major ecosystems; five of the world's seven life zones; three of North America's four desert types; and all kinds of rare, endemic, and protected plant and animal species.

As you gaze out from the rim, you're viewing 2 billion years of geologic history, exposed for all to see in the canyon's rock walls. There's more Paleozoic and Pre-Cambrian earth history on view here than anywhere else on the planet. Far below the rim, the Colorado River continues its timeless carving process. It's been estimated that, prior to the completion of Glen Canyon Dam, an average of 400,000 tons of silt was carried away every day, the equivalent of 80,000 5-ton dump-truck loads—one per second, nonstop.

The Grand Canyon is as vast as its name implies. If you were to travel from one end of the canyon to the other, you would journey just under 280 mi from Lees Ferry near the junction of the Paria and Colorado rivers in northern Arizona to the western border shared by Arizona and Nevada. At its deepest point, the canyon is nearly 6,000 feet. From the North Rim to the South Rim, the distance across varies from 18 mi to less than ½ mi. However, to travel between rims by car requires a journey of 200 mi.

This gaping chasm was dismissed by the first Europeans to come across the sublime spectacle. More than 350 years passed before the canyon became recognized as a natural treasure, receiving federal protection as a forest reserve and then later as a national monument. However, it wasn't until 1919, three years after the creation of the National Park Service, that the Grand Canyon achieved national-park status. Only 44,173 people visited the park that first year.

Park Passes

CLOSE UP

The Grand Canyon National Park Annual Pass, available for $50, gives unlimited access to the park for 12 months from the purchase date. However, your best bet is the America the Beautiful–National Parks and Federal Recreational Lands Pass (☎ 888/275–8747, Ext. 1; ⊕ http://store.usgs.gov/pass), available for $80, which gives unlimited access to all federal recreation areas and national parks for 12 months from pur-chase date. The America the Beautiful Senior Pass has the same benefits for U.S. citizens age 62 or older for the cost of $10. As of January 2007, The America the Beautiful–National Parks and Recreational Lands Pass replaces all previous national-park passes, includ-ing the Golden Eagle Passport, Golden Eagle Hologram, Golden Access Passport, and Golden Age Passport.

Today, nearly 5 million people flock to see the grandeur of the world's most majestic gorge. "Leave it as it is," President Teddy Roosevelt proclaimed. "You cannot improve on it. Keep it for your children, your children's children, and for all who come after you as the one great sight which every American should see."

HISTORY OF THE PARK

Long before the first Europeans stood on the southern rim of the Grand Canyon, Americans Indians roamed the vast Colorado Plateau and the deep canyon chasms. More than 10,000 years ago, prehistoric Paleo-Indians—nomadic peoples known as Elephant Hunters, whose existence depended upon hunting large prehistoric elephants, mast-odons, and mammoths—wandered the Grand Canyon as its first residents.

Then, about 1,500 years ago, the Ancestral Puebloan people—more popularly known as the Anasazi (a name that means both "ancient ones" and "enemy ancestors")— arrived on the scene. They built permanent community complexes and developed agriculture both on and below the rim. More than 2,000 of their sites have been found, including Tusayan Pueblo, some 3 mi west of Desert View on the South Rim, and at Walhalla Glades Pueblo, located near the end of Cape Royal Road on the North Rim. In the late 13th century this culture mysteriously picked up and left the area; anthropologists believe these peoples are the ancestors of the Hopi Indians who live on three mesas to the east.

The last of the Native Americans to occupy the region were the Navajo, who came into the area some 600 years ago and now live on a large reservation to the east of the national park. To the west of the national park, the Havasupai and Hualapai live on reservations encompassing only a small portion of their native lands.

The first Europeans to view the canyon were Spanish Conquistadors, who were more interested in finding the fabled Cibola, the Seven Cities of Gold. Don García López de Cárdenas's band of soldiers spent four days vainly searching for a path to the bottom of the canyon. They were not able to reach the Colorado River to obtain the water they desperately needed and left, uninspired and disappointed. Over 200 years passed before two Spanish priests became the second party of Europeans to see the canyon.

The first recorded Americans to visit the region were an army survey party seeking an alternate southern supply route to Utah. They, too, left in despair and recorded that the canyon was of dubious value. Then, in 1869, John Wesley Powell undertook a famous voyage down the Colorado that created the first everlasting interest in the Grand Canyon.

In the late 19th century prospectors flocked to the canyon in search of mineral resources. Before long, the Grand Canyon's pioneers discovered that the real riches came from tourism. In 1901, the Grand Canyon Railway brought its first load of tourists to the South Rim and development quickly followed. In 1908 the area was declared a national monument, and in 1919 Congress passed legislation making it a national park.

Today, nearly 5 million people each year stand in awe at the canyon and leave with the realization that they have witnessed nature at her finest.

GEOLOGY OF THE PARK

Considered one of the 7 natural wonders of the world, the Grand Canyon stretches along 277 mi of the Colorado River and ranges in width from 4- to 18-mi wide. Nearly 2 billion years of geologic history is revealed in exposed layers cut up to 1-mi deep in the Colorado Plateau.

Upon first exploring the Grand Canyon, one-armed Civil War veteran John Wesley Powell said, "The river was the saw which cut the mountain in two." However, the Colorado River is only one part of the equation. Seventy million years ago, the plate-tectonic events that formed the Rocky Mountains also uplifted the Colorado Plateau thousands of feet higher than the surrounding countryside, setting the stage for the canyon's creation.

It wasn't until five to six million years ago that the Colorado River began to carve the canyon. Almost all of the runoff from the northern edge of the plateau flows south toward the Grand Canyon, meeting up with the Colorado River and its tributaries. The arid landscape paired with the high elevation combined to create an unusual terrain vulnerable to forces of erosion. Under wind and water, the shale layers eroded into slopes and the harder sandstone and limestone layers created terraced cliffs, resulting in the canyon profile seen today.

The rocky pages of history, revealed in the Grand Canyon, range from the 2-billion-year-old Vishnu Schist found at the canyon bottom to the 270-million-year-old Kaibab Limestone on the rims. The oldest rocks lie more than 3,000 feet beneath the rim in the Inner Gorge. The most recent geologic additions to the canyon are igneous rocks deposited during a period of volcanic activity about a million years ago.

Unlike the overlying sedimentary layers, the Vishnu basement rocks are made up of ancient metamorphic formations created by intense heat and pressure deep within earth. The upper layers formed during times of deposition—shallow seas and desert dunes shifting back and forth, leaving layers of weathered sand and silt in their wake.

Not all of the earth's history is present in the tiered layers found in the Grand Canyon. Some layers eroded before new layers were deposited, creating unconformities in the geologic strata. The Great Unconformity, representing 1.2

billion years of missing rock, is the most notable of these gaps in geologic history. Although much of the canyon's origins are known, there are still many questions to be answered by the geologic research of generations to come.

FLORA

Almost two billion years' worth of the earth's history is written in the colored layers of sedimentary rock stacked from the river bottom to the top of the plateau, and more than 1,700 species of plants further color the park. The South Rim's Coconino Plateau is fairly flat, at an elevation of about 7,000 feet, and is covered with stands of pinyon and ponderosa pine, juniper, and Gambel's oak. Douglas-fir, spruce, quaking-aspen, and more ponderosa-pine trees dominate the vegetation on the North Rim's Kaibab Plateau. In the Inner Canyon, seeps and springs support hanging gardens replete with flowering redbud trees and crimson monkeyflower. On the sunny stretches of both rims, you will see high desert plants such as banana yucca and claret-cup cactus. In spring, and if the rains have cooperated, you're likely to see a variety of wildflowers in bloom at both rims.

Banana Yucca *(Yucca baccata)*: Named for the large fleshy fruit it produces in summer, this widespread desert plant can be found on both rims, but is more predominant on the drier South Rim. Banana yuccas put up a dense stalk of creamy white flowers, which bloom anytime between April and June, depending on the elevation. All parts of this plant are used by Southwestern Indian tribes: the fibrous leaves are used to make rope, baskets, and cloth; the roots are used to make soap; and the fruits are eaten raw, roasted, or dried.

Catclaw Acacia *(Acacia greggii)*: Also known as Devil's Claw, this Southwestern native can commonly be found in semi-desert grasslands and brushy rangeland in deep arroyos. The grey-green leaves on this large shrub, which occasionally develops into a small tree, are drought deciduous and lack leaves in the dry season. Its numerous hooked thorns readily catch on clothes, skin, and hair at the slightest touch. Catclaw acacia bloom in May; the fragrant, cream-colored flowers provide fabulous nectar for honey production. Historically, Southwestern tribes used the leaves and roots for medicinal purposes and the legumes from the seed pods as food.

Claret Cups Hedgehog *(Echinocereus triglochidiatus)*: Unlike most of its cactus cousins, claret cup hedgehogs can survive winters at elevations up to 9,000 feet. Found on both rims of the Grand Canyon, this hardy hedgehog blooms with bright-red flowers each spring. The trumpet-shaped flowers attract hummingbirds, instead of bees, for pollination.

Cliffrose *(Cowania mexicana)*: This large, upright shrub, which can grow as tall as 25 feet high, can be found thriving in pinyon-juniper woodland and below the rim on open, rocky slopes. This evergreen member of the rose family puts forth a showy display of white blooms from March through September.

Colorado Pinyon *(Pinus edulis)*: Colorado pinyon is the most common pine-tree species found in the widespread pinyon-juniper woodlands on the Colorado Plateau. Thriving in habitats ranging from 4,000 to 8,000 feet, this popular tree can be found on both rims of the Grand Canyon, but are more abundant at higher elevations. Southwestern tribes harvested pinyon-pine seeds for food and used its rot-resistant wood in construction.

Creosote *(Larrea tridentate)*: Abundant in Southwestern deserts, this evergreen shrub bears dark-green, resinous leaves and can be found covering large areas of well-drained flatland. The pungent leaves repel herbivores with their bitter resin, which also protects the greenery against water loss and sunburn. At least 49 kinds of volatile oils can be found in a creosote stand. These oils give the plant its characteristic odor, which becomes even more pronounced after the first summer rains. In spring, this bush puts forth a blaze of bright-yellow flowers. Creosote bushes have the uncanny ability to clone, splitting off as perfect replicas of the original plant; in the Mohave Desert a ring of genetically identical creosote bushes carbon date more than 10,000 years old.

Crimson Monkeyflower *(Mimulus cardinalis)*: A member of the snapdragon family, the crimson monkeyflower grows 10 to 36 inches tall in upright clumps along shady seeps and springs and permanently running streams. Sporting large, dark-green leaves, this showy flower blooms a bright red between March and October. It can be found at Dripping Springs, Pipe Creek, and Ribbon Falls—all of which are accessible by foot on corridor trails. Deeper in the canyon, large populations of these brightly-colored blooms can be found at Vasey's Paradise, Elves Chasm, and lower Havasu Canyon.

Engelmann Spruce *(Picea engelmannii)*: Found in the upper reaches of the Kaibab Plateau, the Engelmann spruce is one of the tallest trees on the North Rim. Living up to 600 years, this hardy tree stands up to 160 feet tall with a trunk diameter of about 40 inches. Found in elevations exceeding 8,000 feet, it prefers a humid, alpine habitat with long, cold winters and short, cool summers.

Four-wing Saltbush *(Atriplex canescens)*: Named after its four-winged seed, this small shrub is commonly found in pinyon-juniper woodland habitats. Thriving in alkaline soil, this hardy shrub is covered with clusters of small, grayish-green leaves. Tiny yellow flowers decorate the spiky branches from mid-spring to mid-summer. In autumn, the large, four-winged seeds cloak the plant. In the past, Southwestern Indians harvested the seeds and leaves for food.

Hill's Lupine *(Lupinus hillii)*: The most common of the nine species of lupine in the park, this dark purplish-blue wildflower blooms from June through August on both rims. Hill's lupine can only be found in central and northern Arizona and can be distinguished by the dense, colorful clusters of flowers on the 8-inch stalks. Lupines play an important role in the pinyon-juniper woodlands and sagebrush flats by fixing nitrogen in the otherwise rather sterile soil. Hill's lupine can usually be found blooming in Grand Canyon Village and at Yaki Point on the South Rim; and on Transept Trail on the North Rim and in many of the mountain meadows in the Kaibab Forest.

Indian Paintbrush *(Castilleja)*: There are about 200 species of this bright-red, perennial wildflower, which is also known as Prairie-fire. This semiparasitic plant depends on host grasses and other plants to supply water and nutrients. The flowers themselves are inconspicuous—it's the fire-red bracts beneath each flower that draws the eye.

Ponderosa Pine *(Pinus ponderosa)*: Ponderosa-pine forests dominate the upper elevations of the far-flung Colorado Plateau. This stand of ponderosa pines is the largest of its kind in the world. The predominant subspecies in the Kaibab Forest is the three-needled, Rocky Mountain ponderosa pine. The tassel-eared Abert's squirrel on the

South Rim and the Kaibab squirrel on the North Rim are distinct year-round residents in these coniferous forests. Abert's squirrels are dependent on ponderosa pines for food and shelter.

Utah Juniper *(Juniperus osteosperma)*: Of the six species found in Arizona, Utah juniper is the most common juniper found on the Colorado Plateau. The presence of this small, gnarled tree is an indicator of a pinyon-juniper pygmy forest, which is prevalent on the South Rim. This evergreen tree rarely grows taller than 15 feet and is easily recognizable by its spiny, branched fronds; powder-coated, bluish-gray berries; and easily shredded, grayish-brown bark. Southwestern tribes have historically collected mature juniper berries for food. The reddish-brown seed in the berry is harvested by the Navajo, who string these "ghost beads" together in necklaces and bracelets.

Western Redbud *(Cercis occidentalis)*: This showy, small tree thrives near seeps and springs in the inner corridors of the Grand Canyon. It only reaches a maximum height of 12 feet, but its clusters of red-purple flowers makes it one of the most colorful canyon inhabitants. Twigs and branches break out in bloom in early to mid-April, followed by the appearance of large, rounded leaves in late April. Long, flat seed pods show up by mid-May, turning brown late in the summer. The Bright Angel Trail, along the creek at Indian Gardens, is a good place to see blooming redbuds.

FAUNA

Eighty-nine mammal species inhabit the park, as do 355 species of birds, 56 kinds of reptiles and amphibians, and 17 kinds of fish. The rare Kaibab squirrel is found only on the North Rim, and the pink Grand Canyon rattlesnake lives at lower elevations within the canyon. Hawks and ravens are visible year-round, usually coasting on the wind above the canyon. The endangered California condor has been reintroduced to the canyon. In summer, park rangers give daily talks on the magnificent birds, whose wing-span measures 9 feet. In spring, summer, and fall mule deer are abundant, even aggressive, at the South Rim. Don't be tempted to feed them: it's illegal, and it will disrupt their natural habits and increase your risk of being bitten.

Abert's Squirrel *(Sciurus aberti)*: This tassel-eared squirrel resides in coniferous forests, typically building its nests in

Bringing Your Pets

Pets are allowed in Grand Canyon National Park; however, they must be on a leash at all times. With the exception of service animals, pets are not allowed in park lodgings, on shuttle buses, or most park trails. On the South Rim, pets are allowed on the trails above the rim, Mather Campground, Desert View Campground, Trailer Village, and throughout the developed areas. On the North Rim, the only rim trail accessible to pets is the Bridle Trail, which connects Grand Canyon Lodge with the North Kaibab Trail. There is a kennel at the Maswik Transportation Center (☎ 928/638–0534) on the South Rim; there is no kennel on the North Rim. Persons wishing to take a service animal below the rim must check-in first at the Backcountry Information Center (☎ 928/638–7875). Pets are not allowed at Grand Canyon West or in Havasu Canyon.

the branches of ponderosa pine. Unlike other squirrels, the Abert's squirrel doesn't store food for the winter. Instead it feeds upon ponderosa-pine seeds and buds in the summer and parts of the tree's inner bark in the winter. This perky critter is named after American naturalist Colonel John James Abert, who helped map the American West in the early 1800s.

American Black Bear *(Ursus americanus)*: In the Southwest, black bears prefer to live in forested areas and thrive in pinyon-juniper habitats. They usually range in length from 5 to 6 feet long, standing about 3 feet at the shoulder. They can stand and walk on their hindquarters, but usually shuffle along on all fours. These bears sport a shaggy black or chocolate-brown coat and have a long snout, which gives them an excellent sense of smell. Opportunistic eaters, black bears dine on a variety of foods, including insects, nuts, berries, fish, and small mammals.

American Crow *(Corvus brachyrhynchos)*: Characterized as a trickster by many Southwestern Native American tribes, the American crow lives up to its reputation with its curious nature and the ability to mimic sounds made by other animals and birds. It is also one of the few birds ever observed using tools to obtain food. This distinctive, black bird is smaller than the common raven and can often be seen riding the winds between canyon walls.

Bald Eagle *(Haliaeetus leucocephalus)*: The national bird of the United States, this large raptor lives near large bodies of water and prefers to nest in old-growth trees. This distinct eagle has a dark brown body with a snowy white head and tail. Males and females have the same plumage, but the females are about 25% larger. Their primary food is fish, but they will prey on ducks and other birds as well. More than two dozen bald eagles winter in the Colorado River corridor, with the highest concentrations found near Nankoweap Creek.

Black-tailed Jackrabbit *(Lepus californicus)*: Also known as a desert hare, this jackrabbit has long ears and powerful legs. Reaching about 2 feet in length and weighing up to 6 pounds, this jumpy critter is the third largest rabbit in North America. Black-tipped ears and a black-tail stripe mark its buff-colored coat. When startled, it can jump as high as 19 feet and reach speed of up to 45 mi an hour. This desert dweller primarily eats cactus, juniper berries, wild grass, sagebrush, and mesquite. It is usually nocturnal, but can often be seen in the early morning and late afternoon hours.

Bobcat *(Lynx rufus)*: This North American feline is about twice the size of a domestic cat and lives in woodlands and high desert habitats. Bobcats have grayish-brown coats, black-tufted ears, and a short black-tipped tail. They prey primarily on rabbits, but are also known to eat insects, rodents, birds, squirrels, and even deer. Solitary and territorial, bobcats are crepuscular and can occasionally be spotted at dawn or at twilight.

Burrowing Owl *(Athene cunicularia)*: This diminutive owl nests and roosts in abandoned prairie-dog burrows. They are distinctive in appearance with their bright-yellow eyes and bills, flattened-facial disks, and prominent white eyebrows. This droll owl sports a white breast and belly with brown barring and brown backs dotted with white speckles. Unlike most owls, burrowing owls are often active during the day, even though most hunting is done at night.

Cactus Wren *(Campylorhynchus brunneicapillus)*: At 7 to 9 inches in length, the cactus wren is the largest of the nine wrens found in the United States. It can be identified by its brown head, barred wings and tail, white-eye stripe, and spotted-tail feathers. The cactus wren thrives primarily on insects, but will also eat seeds and fruit. This desert dweller is a native of the Southwest and nests in cactuses, yucca, and thorny bushes. Cactus wrens are territorial and mate for life. It is the Arizona state bird.

California Condor *(Gymnogyps californianus)*: Teetering on the brink of extinction, California condors soar through the Grand Canyon as part of one of the most intensive conservations projects in United States history. The largest flying land bird in North America, this opportunistic scavenger feeds exclusively on large dead mammals. They have a wingspan stretching nearly 10 feet and can glide at speeds up to 50 mi an hour. They are easily identifiable with their bald, pinkish-orange heads; curved, ivory bills; and black feathered bodies marked with white, triangular wing patches. They can live up to 60 years in the wild. The first six California condors were reintroduced to the Vermillion Cliffs in 1996. Today, more than 60 condors fly Arizona's skies. The best places to view California condors in the Grand Canyon are at the South Rim in the summer and near the Colorado River in Marble Canyon in the winter. California condors can be seen year-round at Vermillion Cliffs.

Collared Peccary *(Tayassu tajuca)*: Collared peccaries, better known as javelinas, can be commonly found in desert scrub along creeks, arroyos, and at the canyon mouths of mountain ranges. Adults sport a jaunty salt-and-pepper coat with a dark mane of bristles, which rise when the animals are startled, giving them a larger appearance than their standard height of 19 inches and 60-pound frame. Herds forage together for a variety of food, including prickly pear fruit and pads; tuberous roots; fishhook and hedgehog cacti; agave; and the seeds of palo verde, jojoba, catclaw and juniper. Because they are sensitive to heat and cold, javelinas are nocturnal in the summer; in the winter they reverse the process.

Coyote *(Canis latrans)*: Coyotes thrive throughout the Southwest in a variety of habitats, from the low Sonoran Desert floor to the high forested mountains. Reddish-gray with a buff underside, coyotes resemble medium-sized dogs, but their yellow eyes; alert ears; and bushy, black-tipped tails give away their wild nature. They run in packs or as loners, roam either day or night, and eat nearly anything: fresh meat, carrion, insects, fruits, and vegetables. Coyotes exercise a diverse vocal repertoire filled with barks, wails, and yips. In the Southwest, coyotes are more often heard than seen, sometimes congregating in "choir lofts" to serenade the moon.

Desert Big Horn Sheep *(Ovis canadensis)*: Desert bighorn sheep are known for their rugged aggressiveness, tenacious footwork, and their ability to survive in inhospitable landscapes. Desert bighorn sheep get most of their moisture from plants and dew. However, when they come across a water source, they can drink up to 2 gallons of water in just a few minutes, which they can then store in their enlarged stomach compartments for several days. Both rams and ewes sport spiraling horns, but the rams' horns are double the size, measuring up to 30 to 40 inches along the outside curl, and weigh up to 30 pounds. Aggressive when competing for the ewes, the rams engage in head-to-head combat, which has been observed to last as long as 24 hours.

Desert Tortoise *(Gopherus agassizii)*: Native to Southwestern deserts, this tortoise spends the majority of its lifetime in burrows. They can grow up to 2 feet in length and have thick, stubby legs ending in heavy claws used for digging. They live in sandy flats and rocky washes in elevations up to 3,500 feet. This slow-moving tortoise eats grasses, wildflowers, shrubs, and cactus flower and fruit. Most of its moisture intake comes from its food; they can live up to a year without drinking water. Desert tortoises are protected by state and federal law.

Eastern Collared Lizard *(Crotaphytus collaris)*: This colorful critter lives in dry, rocky habitats across most of the southern states and down into Mexico. Depending on their environment, these reptiles vary in color from a plain grayish-tan to a flashy cobalt blue. However, all of them share in common the double black bands around their slim necks from which they earned their name. Territorial and aggressive by nature, these rapacious reptiles prefer to chomp on other lizards, including their own kind. During May and June, the normally dull females signal their readiness to mate by turning the color of an Arizona sunset with vivid red or orange stripes on their sides and tails.

Elk *(Cervus canadensis)*: Ranking as the second-largest species of deer in the world, this wide-ranging mammal lives in forest habitats and feeds on grasses, plants, leaves, and bark. During the summer, elk graze almost constantly and will consume as much as 15 pounds of food in one day. They have dark reddish-brown coats with a characteristic white rump patch. Males sport large antlers, which they use when competing with other males during mating season. Their bugling mating call is one of the most distinctive sounds of autumn.

Gila Monster *(Heloderma suspectum)*: This large, venomous lizard is native to the Southwest and can easily be identified by its intricately patterned, yellow- and black-studded scales. Gila monsters can reach up to 2 feet in length and survive on a menu of rodents, birds, and eggs. They live in burrows and can be found in rocky foothills at elevations up to 4,800 feet. Gila monsters are listed as a threatened species and are protected under state and federal law.

Gila Woodpecker *(Melanerpes chrysaetos)*: The Gila woodpecker is distinguished from other woodpeckers by the black-and-white zebra stripes on its back and grayish-tan throat and belly. It also sports white wing patches, which are visible in flight. Males have an added splash of color with the red cap on their heads. This desert dweller feeds primarily on insects, but supplements its diet with nuts, berries, fruit, invertebrates, and seeds. Noisy by nature, Gila woodpeckers are especially notorious for their drumming.

Grand Canyon Rattlesnake *(Crotalus oreganus abyssus)*: Of the six species of rattlesnakes found in the park, the Grand Canyon pink rattlesnake is the most common. This subspecies of the western diamondback is only found in the Grand Canyon and connecting side canyons. This venomous snake averages about 2 to 3 feet in length and is a light pinkish-tan color. It is nocturnal during the hottest part of the summer and hibernates in the winter. It feeds on rodents, lizards, and birds and is most often seen in the spring and fall during the early morning and late afternoon.

Gray Fox *(Urocyon cinereoargenteus)*: This member of the canid family is primarily nocturnal, but sometimes can be seen foraging during the day. This small fox has grayish-brown fur, sports a white belly and facial markings, and has a black stripe on its back and tail. It can climb trees and feeds on small mammals, insects, birds, eggs, nuts, and berries.

Great Horned Owl *(Bubo virginianus)*: The largest owl in North America, the great horned owl ranges in length from 18 to 27 inches with a wingspan of 49 inches. Their disc-shaped face acts like a radar dish, catching faint sounds in a wide range of frequencies. The owl's hearing is so acute, it generally locates its prey in the dark undergrowth by sound alone, perching and hooting to panic the mice and rabbits into betraying their position. This nocturnal predator can see well in dim light and can swivel its head 270 degrees, which gives it wider range of motion to detect prey without moving and giving away its position. This and the owl's ability for ghostly flight make it a most successful predator.

Greater Roadrunner *(Geococcyx californianus)*: The roadrunner, a denizen of the lower Sonoran Desert, tends to stay in the sagebrush flatlands, but isolated wanderers have been spotted at elevations of 10,000 feet. The roadrunner resembles a hen pheasant, but is distinguished by a bright-orange patch of bare skin behind its eyes, which is sometimes obscured, and a crest of black and bronze-green feathers that rise and lower, depending on emotion. Roadrunners measure just 22 to 24 inches in length, half of which is tail. This opportunistic and voracious omnivore eats everything from insects and berries to lizards and snakes. The roadrunner earned his name when settlers traveling westward first discovered that this vivacious bird liked to race their wagons.

Humpback Chub *(Gila cypha)*: This very rare, endangered fish lives in deep, turbid waters. The high hump on its back helps it pass under rushing waters, keeping it near the river bottom where the currents aren't as swift. This protected species is distinguished by its streamlined body, overhanging mouth, and pronounced hump. Historically found throughout the Colorado River and its tributaries, it is now only found in the Little Colorado River and adjacent portions of the Colorado River.

Kaibab Squirrel *(Sciurus aberti kaibabensis)*: This tassel-eared squirrel lives exclusively in the ponderosa-pine forests on the Kaibab Plateau. Kaibab squirrels are related to the Abert's squirrel on the South Rim, but have evolved into their own subspecies due to the geographic isolation created by the Grand Canyon. The brownish-black Kaibab squirrel is distinguished by its bushy white tail and long tufted ears. Like other tassel-eared squirrels, it feeds primarily on ponderosa-pine seeds, bark, and twigs, but supplements its diet with nuts, fruit, and fungi.

Mountain Lion *(Puma concolor)*: Also called a cougar or a puma, the mountain lion is a large, solitary cat and an important predator in keeping deer populations stable on the Kaibab Plateau. Although it resembles a domestic cat, this territorial feline usually weighs between 100 to 160 pounds and is about 8 feet long from nose to tail. Their tan coat is broken with light patches of fur on its face, throat, and belly. It is seldom seen and typically avoids humans.

Mule Deer *(Odocoileus hemionus)*: A frequent sight on the Kaibab Plateau, mule deer are named for their large trademark ears. The bucks weigh up to 300 pounds and sport forked antlers. Does are considerably smaller and average anywhere from 100 to 175 pounds. Both sexes are tan and have black-tipped tails. In the early 1900s, a bounty seriously depleted the number of natural predators on the Kaibab Plateau, and as a result, deer populations exploded from about 4,000 animals in 1907 to more than 100,000 animals in 1924. Overgrazed rangelands led to a climatic crash in mule-deer population. In the decades that followed, the natural order finally returned. Today, there are 8,000 deer roaming the plateau woodlands and mountain meadows.

Porcupine *(Erethizon dorsatum)*: Porcupines live in a wide variety of habitats including deserts, forests, and grass-lands. This large rodent is ungainly, but makes a sharp impression with its suit of spines; the barbed quills detach as a defense mechanism. They come in various shades of brown and gray and can often be seen in treetops and alongside the road.

Ringtail *(Bassariscus astutus)*: This nocturnal member of the raccoon family is dark brown, has a white-masked feline face, and black and white-striped tail that is longer than its body. It is smaller than an ordinary housecat and lives a solitary life in its forest habitat. Ringtails are omnivo-rous and exist on a diet of fruit, berries, lizards, birds, and rodents. They are rarely seen, but have been known to sneak into historic-park structures for a look at the action. The ringtail is the Arizona state mammal.

Violet-green Swallow *(Tachycineta thalassina)*: Nesting in canyon cliffs, this flashy bird catches the attention of visi-tors with it acrobatic flights. This athletic avian sports iri-descent violet-green feathers with pearly-white undersides and facial markings. They are only about 5 inches long and feed almost exclusively on flying insects.

Western Pipistrelle *(Pipistrellus herperus)*: The smallest bat known to inhabit North America, the western pipistrelle weighs in at a mere 3 to 6 grams—just slightly more than a penny—and will barely fill a human hand, even with its wings spread. Noted for their golden fur, black-face mask and large eyes, these tiny bats can be seen searching for prey—flies, moths, small beetles, mosquitoes, and flying ants—as early as two hours before sundown. They prefer to roost in narrow rocky cliffside crevices. Even though these little critters can be easily buffeted by strong winds, they are known for their hardiness and tenacity—proving, perhaps, that bigger isn't always better in the world of bats.

Wild Turkey (*Meleagris gallopavo*): Of the six subspecies of wild turkey, Merriam's turkey inhabits the pine forests and mountain meadows on the Kaibab Plateau. Named after 20th-century biologist C. Hart Merriam, this turkey sports a dark-brown body, glossy purplish-bronze wings, and white-tipped tail feathers. Like their domesticated counterparts, they have a small bald head with fleshy caruncles. Males have red wattles on their necks. They travel in small groups and roost at night in trees.

IF YOU LIKE

BICYCLING

Rangers say the best bet for mountain bikers is the Rainbow Rim Trail, which goes along the North Rim of the canyon along a ponderosa-pine forest and up and down through side canyons, aspen groves, and pristine meadows. Mountain bikers heading to the North Rim will enjoy testing the many dirt access roads found in this remote area, including the 17-mi trek to Point Sublime. It's a rarity to spot other people on these primitive roads. On the other hand, bikers wanting to see the South Rim of the Grand Canyon on two wheels might be disappointed by the experience because of narrow shoulders on park roads and the heavy traffic. Bicycles are prohibited on park trails with the exception of the Greenway System, currently under development on the South Rim, so the off-road biking is also limited here. Mountain bikers visiting the South Rim may be better off meandering through the ponderosa-pine forest on the Tusayan Bike Trail.

CAMPING

Camping on both rims of Grand Canyon National Park is confined to developed campgrounds: Desert View and

Tips for RVers

Of the three campgrounds within park boundaries on the South Rim, only Trailer Village can accommodate RVs over 30 feet long. It is also the only one with hookups. The limited number of sites paired with the high demand makes these RV sites hard to come by. Reservations (☎ 888/297–2757) should be made at least five months in advance. With the heavy congestion on South Rim roads, RV travelers should plan to park and get around using the park's extensive shuttle system. A better bet is to visit the canyon during the slower, serene winter months when sites are available on a first-come, first-served basis. The more remote North Rim offers a limited number of RV sites at its one park campground. However, campers willing to do without services can get settled at one of the hundreds of dispersed camping sites located throughout the Kaibab National Forest (☎ 928/643-7298), which surrounds the national park's northern boundaries. Some of these sites are located just a short walk's distance from Eastern Rim viewpoints.

Mather campgrounds on the South Rim and the North Rim Campground on the Kaibab Plateau. Maintained campgrounds below the rim on the main-corridor trails include Cottonwood, Bright Angel, and Indian campgrounds. Ten-X is the only developed campground in the Kaibab National Forest Tusayan Ranger District near the South Rim. Developed national-forest-camping sites near the North Rim in the North Kaibab Ranger District include Demotte, Indian Hollow, and Jacob Lake campgrounds. For a more relaxed experience, pitch your tent in one of the more remote and less accessible campsites found throughout the inner canyon backcountry, or at the dispersed campsites scattered throughout the Kaibab National Forest.

FAMILY FUN

The Junior Ranger Program at Grand Canyon National Park provides a free, fun way to look at the cultural and natural history of this sublime destination. These hands-on educational programs for children ages 4 to 14 include guided adventure hikes, ranger-led "discovery" programs, and book readings. The paved Rim Trail is perfect for families looking to stretch their legs at the South Rim. The North Rim has several kid-friendly rim hikes including Cape Royal, Cliff Springs, Roosevelt Point, and Transept trails. The Kaibab National Forest Visitors Center in Jacob Lake also offers a kids' program complete with educational displays and children's activities.

GAZING AT THE SCENERY

The best times to see the canyon are during the hours just after dawn and just before dusk. The shifting light brightens the canyon walls in chromatic bands of gold, violet, maroon, copper, salmon, and indigo. Instead of jostling with crowds on the popular South Rim viewpoints, head to the less visited North Rim—or take a short hike into the canyon for views at the Coconino Overlook on the North Kaibab Trail, or at Ooh Aah Point on the South Kaibab Trail.

HIKING

Hikers can choose from a plethora of canyon trails including everything from an easy rim hike to an arduous journey into the depths of this massive gorge. Even though an immense network of trails winds through the Grand Canyon, the popular corridor trails are recommended for the first overnight trip in the canyon for hikers new to the region. Hiking steep trails from rim to rim is a strenuous trek of at least 21 mi and should only be attempted by experienced canyon hikers. Although permits are not required for day hikes, you must have a backcountry permit for longer trips. Some of the more popular paths and trails are listed in this book, and more detailed information and maps can be obtained from the Backcountry Information Center.

WHITE-WATER ADVENTURES

Upon first entering the Grand Canyon in 1869, explorer John Wesley Powell said, "We are now ready to start . . . down the Great Unknown." Since that time, the innermost depths of the Grand Canyon have been extensively mapped along the Colorado River. However, this remote region is still an unknown wonder to most Grand Canyon visitors who peer down at the mighty river from a lofty viewpoint thousands of feet above its steady course. More than a dozen companies offer white-water adventures down the Colorado River from Lees Ferry to Diamond Creek. Side hikes to Indian ruins and stops at secluded waterfalls only add to the magical journey. Motorized trips take about seven days, but shorter three- to four-day trips are available for rafters willing to hike in or out of the canyon at

Phantom Ranch. A less strenuous, one-day trip is offered by the Hualapai River Runners on the West Rim.

WILDLIFE-WATCHING

Encompassing habitats ranging from desert lowlands to alpine forests, Grand Canyon National Park is an important wildlife preserve. With more than 500 animal species living within park boundaries, there are nearly limitless opportunities for wildlife viewing. The best times to see wildlife are early in the morning and late in the afternoon. Look for out-of-place shapes and motions, keeping in mind that animals occupy all of the layers in a natural habitat. Use binoculars for close-up views. While out and about try to fade into the woodwork by keeping your movements limited and noise at a minimum. Never feed wild animals in the national park. Not only is it dangerous—it's illegal.

Exploring the South Rim

WORD OF MOUTH

"When we were there we viewed the sunset from the main area outside Bright Angel lodge—beautiful! We caught the sunrise from the South Kaibab trailhead—beautiful! Storm rolled in that night, no sunset just thunder and lightning—awesome! Next day, cloudy, misty, light rain, sun peeking though clouds—beautiful! I guess what I am saying is don't get too hung up on being at the right spot for the sunrise/sunset, it's all spectacular!"

—BlackandGold

By Carrie
Miner

WHEN LT. JOSEPH IVES VISITED THE SOUTH RIM of the Grand Canyon on an exploratory U.S. War Department expedition in 1857, he declared it to be "altogether value-less." "Ours has been the first and will doubtless be the last party of whites to visit this profitless locality," Ives remarked. "It seems intended by nature that the Colorado River, along the greater portion of its lonely and majestic way, shall be forever unvisited and undisturbed."

He was wrong. Of the nearly 5 million people who visit the Grand Canyon each year, 4 million throng the South Rim's lodges, restaurants, and breathtaking viewpoints. Visiting during peak summer weekends and holidays requires patience and a tolerance for crowds. Even while jostling for a spot at the most popular viewpoints, most visitors are enthralled by the sheer scope of the deepest, most stunning canyon on the planet. Visiting in the off-season—including winter, when the snow mantles the landscape and contrasts with the reds, oranges, yellows, blues, and purples of the canyon—offers a more intimate experience.

Most people don't give the canyon enough time, flitting quickly from viewpoint to viewpoint near the main lodge in a fit of drive-by sightseeing. Many drive to the main visitor center then take the 25-mi Desert View Drive, which follows the rim and offers frequent viewpoints. But even during the peak times you can find some solitude from the pressing crowds. A bus shuttles passengers to the less-visited and less-crowded viewpoints to the west of the main lodge. You can also walk down several different trails from various viewpoints, although the steep climb and high elevation can pose problems for people who aren't in shape or have heart or respiratory problems.

Another option is to start from the main lodge and stroll along the mostly paved Rim Trail. Crowds drop off sharply as soon as you start walking, even during the busy seasons. Try to arrange your schedule to take in at least one sunrise or sunset. The light of midday flattens even the Grand Canyon, but early and late light make the sandstone cliffs glow and fill the canyon's depths with shadow. The drama of the canyon is enhanced with a glimpse of one of the endangered California condors, which were reintroduced to their historical canyon habitat in 1996. The condors often visit the South Rim, although watchful biologists try to shoo them away to prevent them from getting used to human beings.

WHAT TO SEE

Visitors to the canyon converge mostly on the South Rim, and mostly during the summer. Grand Canyon Village is here, with most of the park's lodging and camping, trailheads, restaurants, stores, and museums, along with a nearby airport and railroad depot. Believe it or not, the average stay in the park is a mere four hours; this is not advised! You need to spend several days to truly appreciate this marvelous place, but at the very least, give it a full day. Hike down into the canyon, or along the rim, to get away from the crowds and experience nature at its finest.

VISITOR CENTERS

Canyon View Information Plaza. The park's main orientation center near Mather Point provides pamphlets and resources to help plan your sightseeing. Park rangers are on hand to answer questions and aid in planning canyon excursions. A bookstore is stocked with books covering all topics on the Grand Canyon, and a daily schedule of ranger-led hikes and evening lectures is posted on a bulletin board inside. The information center can be reached by a short walk from Mather Point, by a short ride on the shuttle bus Village Route, or by a leisurely 1-mi walk on the Greenway Trail. ⊠*East side of Grand Canyon Village* ☏*928/638–7888* ⊙*Daily 8–5, outdoor exhibits may be viewed anytime.*

Desert View Information Center. The information center has a bookstore and is within walking distance of the Watchtower. ⊠*East entrance* ☏*800/858–2808* ⊙*Daily 9–5; hrs vary in winter.*

Yavapai Observation Station. Shop in the bookstore, catch the park shuttle bus, or pick up information for the Rim Trail here. This visitor center also hosts ranger programs, provides expansive views of the canyon, and offers several educational exhibits suitable for all ages. ⊠*1 mi east of Market Plaza* ☏*928/638–7888* ⊙*Mid-May to mid-Oct., daily 8–7; mid-Oct. to mid-May, daily 8–6.*

SCENIC DRIVES

Desert View Drive. This heavily traveled 23-mi stretch of road follows the rim from the east entrance to Grand Canyon Village. Starting from the less-congested entry near

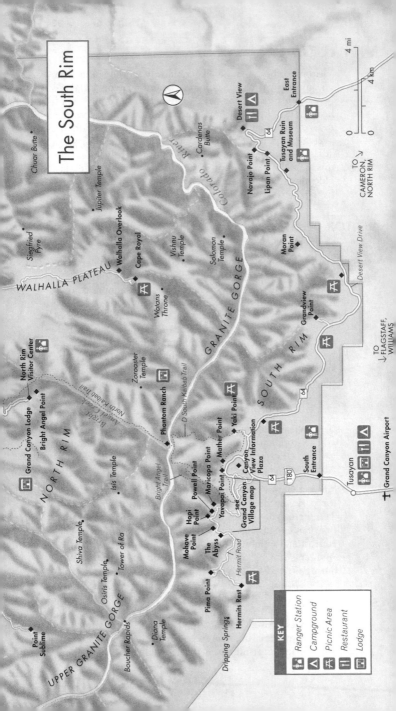

The South Rim

KEY

Ranger Station	
Campground	
Picnic Area	
Restaurant	
Lodge	

4 mi

4 km

0

0

TO CAMERON, NORTH RIM →

TO FLAGSTAFF, WILLIAMS ↓

Desert View

East Entrance

Tusayan Ruin and Museum

Navajo Point

Lipan Point

Moran Point

Grandview Point

Cardenas Butte

Colorado River

GRANITE GORGE

SOUTH RIM

Desert View Drive

C4

C4

180

South Entrance

Tusayan

✝ Grand Canyon Airport

Yaki Point

Mather Point

Canyon View Information Plaza

see Grand Canyon Village map

Maricopa Point

Yavapai Point

Powell Point

Hopi Point

Mohave Point

The Abyss

Pima Point

Hermits Rest

Hermit Road

Bright Angel Trail

South Kaibab Trail

Phantom Ranch

North Kaibab Trail

Bright Angel Creek

NORTH RIM

North Rim Visitor Center

Grand Canyon Lodge

Bright Angel Point

Walhalla Overlook

Cape Royal

WALHALLA PLATEAU

Vishnu Temple

Solomon Temple

Wotans Throne

Zoroaster Temple

Isis Temple

Shiva Temple

Osiris Temple

Tower of Ra

UPPER GRANITE GORGE

Point Sublime

Diana Temple

Boucher Rapids

Dripping Springs

Jupiter Temple

Siegfried Pyre

Chuar Butte

Desert View, road warriors can get their first glimpse of the canyon from the 70-foot-tall Watchtower, the top of which provides the highest viewpoint on the South Rim, before stocking up on maps and information at the Desert View Information Center. Eight overlooks and the ruins of an Anasazi pueblo at the Tusayan Ruin and Museum make this drive a must-do for all visitors to the South Rim. To extend the trip, pack a picnic lunch and stop at the Buggeln picnic area (located 15 mi east of Grand Canyon Village), one of the most secluded and lovely picnic sites on the South Rim.

Hermit Road. The Santa Fe Company built Hermit Road, formerly known as West Rim Drive, in 1912 as a scenic-tour route. Ten overlooks dot this 8-mi stretch, each worth a visit. The road is filled with hairpin turns, so make sure you adhere to posted speed limits. From March through November, Hermit Road is closed to private auto traffic because of congestion; during this period, a free shuttle bus will carry you to all the overlooks. Riding the bus round-trip without getting off at any of the viewpoints takes 75 minutes; the return trip stops only at Mohave and Hopi points. ■TIP➔ **Take plenty of water with you for the ride—the only water along the way is at Hermits Rest.**

AN ALTERNATE ROUTE
Avoid road rage by choosing a different route to the South Rim, foregoing the traditional highways 64 and U.S. 180 from Flagstaff. Take U.S. 89 north from Flagstaff instead, passing near Sunset Crater and Wupatki national monuments. When you reach Cameron Trading Post at the junction with Highway 64, take a break—or stay overnight. This is a good place to shop for Native American artifacts, souvenirs, and the usual postcards, dream-catchers, recordings, and T-shirts. There are also high-quality Navajo rugs, jewelry, and other authentic handicrafts, and you can sample Navajo tacos. U.S. 64 to the west takes you directly to the park's east entrance; the scenery along the Little Colorado River Gorge en route is eye-popping. It's 25 mi from the Grand Canyon east entrance to the visitor center at Canyon View Information Plaza.

HISTORIC SIGHTS

Kolb Studio. Built in 1904 by the Kolb brothers as a photographic workshop and residence, this building provides a view of Indian Gardens, where, in the days before a pipe-

Illuminating Views

Colors deepen dramatically among the contrasting layers of the canyon walls just before and during sunrise and sunset. Hopi Point is the top spot on the South Rim to watch the sun set; Yaki and Pima points also offer vivid views. For a grand sunrise, try Mather or Yaki Points. Arrive at least 30 minutes early for sunrise views and as much as 90 minutes for sunset views. For another point of view, take a leisurely stroll along the Rim Trail and watch the color change along with the views. Timetables are listed in *The Guide*, which you can pick up in any visitor center.

The canyon is actually at its best before 10 am and after 2 pm, when the angle of the sun brings out the colors of the rocks, and clouds and shadows add dimension. "It is never the same, even from day to day, or even from hour to hour. Every passing cloud, every change in the position of the sun, recasts the whole," gushed Clarence Dutton of the U.S. Geological Survey in 1882.

line was installed, Emery Kolb descended 3,000 feet each day to get the water he needed to develop his prints. Kolb was doing something right; he operated the studio until he died in 1976 at age 95. The gallery here has changing exhibitions of paintings, photography, and crafts. There's also a bookstore. During the winter months, a ranger-led tour of the studio illustrates the role the Kolb brothers had on the development of the Grand Canyon. Participation is limited to 12 people; call ahead to sign up for the tour. ⊠ *Grand Canyon Village, near Bright Angel Lodge* ☎928/638–2771 ⊗ *Mid-May–mid-Oct., daily 8–5; mid-Oct.–mid-May, daily 8–6.*

Lookout Studio. Built in 1914 to compete with the Kolbs' photographic studio, the building was designed by architect Mary Jane Colter. The combination lookout point and gift shop has a collection of fossils and geologic samples from around the world. An upstairs loft provides another excellent overlook into the gorge below. ⊠ *About ¼ mi west of Hermit Road Junction on Hermit Rd.* ⊗ *Daily 9–5.*

Powell Memorial. A granite statue honors the memory of John Wesley Powell, who measured, charted, and named many of the canyons and creeks of the Colorado River. It was here that the dedication ceremony for Grand Canyon National Park took place on April 3, 1920. ⊠ *About 3 mi west of Hermit Road Junction on Hermit Rd.*

GREAT ITINERARIES

SOUTH RIM IN 1 DAY

Start early, pack a picnic lunch, and take the shuttle to **Canyon View Information Plaza** just north of the south entrance, to pick up information and see your first incredible view at **Mather Point.** Continue east along **Desert View Drive** for about 2 mi to **Yaki Point,** your first stop. Next, hop back on the shuttle to head 7 mi east to **Grandview Point,** for a good view of the buttes Krishna Shrine and Vishnu Temple. Go 4 mi east and catch the view at **Moran Point,** then 3 mi to the **Tusayan Ruin and Museum,** where a small display is devoted to the history of the Ancestral Puebloans. Continue another mile east to **Lipan Point** to view the Colorado River. In less than 1 mi, you'll arrive at **Navajo Point,** the highest elevation on the South Rim. **Desert View and Watchtower** are the final stops along the shuttle route.

On the return shuttle, hop off at any of the picnic areas for lunch. Walk the paved **Rim Trail** to **Maricopa Point.** Along the way, pick up souvenirs in the village and stop at the historic **El Tovar Hotel** to make dinner reservations. If you have time, take the shuttle on **Hermit Road** to **Hermits Rest,** 8 mi away, to watch the sunset.

SOUTH RIM IN 3 DAYS

On Day 1, follow the one-day itinerary for the morning, but spend more time exploring Desert View Drive and enjoy a leisurely picnic or lunch in Grand Canyon Village. Travel Hermit Road on your second morning, and drive to Grand Canyon Airport for a late morning small plane or helicopter tour of the area. Have lunch in **Tusayan** and cool off during the IMAX film *Grand Canyon: The Hidden Secrets.* Back in the Village, take in a free ranger-led program. On Day 3, take a day hike partway down the canyon on **Bright Angel Trail.** Expect to take twice as long to hike back up. Pick up trail maps at **Canyon View Information Plaza,** and bring plenty of water.

Alternately, spend Day 2 and 3 exploring **Grand Canyon West.** Fill the first day with a Hummer tour along the rim, a helicopter ride into the canyon, or a pontoon-boat ride on the Colorado River; fill up on Hualapai tacos at the Hualapai Lodge's Diamond Creek Restaurant. The next day, raft the Class V and VI rapids or hike 8 mi into **Havasu Canyon** to the small village of Supai and the Havasupai Lodge. You'll need a Havasupai tribal permit to hike here.

2

CLOSE UP

Avoiding Canyon Crowds

It's hard to commune with nature while you're searching for a parking place, dodging video cameras, and stepping away from strollers. However, this scenario is likely to occur only during the very peak months from mid-May through mid-October. Your best bet to beat the crowds is to visit during the off-peak winter and spring seasons.

If you do decide to visit the South Rim during the busy summer and fall months, it's best to leave your car at home. Instead, ride the rails with the Grand Canyon Railway to get to the South Rim; while you're there, utilize the easily accessible shuttles to get from point to point. Travelers can get an even closer look at this natural wonder by going on a day hike—or, for the truly adventurous, on an overnight camping trip into the depths of a canyon. Only about 30,000 visitors apply each year for backcountry permits, a mere fraction of the visitation on both rims.

Tusayan Ruin and Museum. Completed in 1932, the Tusayan Museum offers a quick orientation to the lifestyles of the prehistoric- and modern-Indian populations associated with the Grand Canyon and the Colorado Plateau. Of special interest are split-twig figurines dating back 2,000 to 4,000 years, a 10,000-year-old spear point carved out of chert, and other artifacts left behind by ancient cultures. Adjacent to the museum, an excavation of an 800-year-old ruin gives a glimpse at the lives of some of the Grand Canyon's earliest residents. Twice daily, a ranger leads an interpretive tour of the Ancestral Puebloan village along a 0.1-mi paved loop trail. ⊠*About 20 mi east of Grand Canyon Village on Desert View Dr.* ⊙*Daily 9–5.*

SCENIC STOPS

The Abyss. At an elevation of 6,720 feet, the Abyss is one of the most awesome stops on Hermit Road, revealing a sheer drop of 3,000 feet to the Tonto Platform, a wide terrace of Tapeats sandstone layers about two-thirds of the way down the canyon. From the Abyss you'll also see several isolated sandstone columns, the largest of which is called the Monument. ⊠*About 5 mi west of Hermit Road Junction on Hermit Rd.*

Desert View and Watchtower. From the top of the 70-foot stone and mortar Watchtower, even the muted hues of the distant Painted Desert to the east and the Vermilion Cliffs rising from a high plateau near the Utah border are visible. In the chasm below, angling to the north toward Marble Canyon, an imposing stretch of the Colorado River reveals itself. Up several flights of stairs, the Watchtower houses a glass-enclosed observatory with powerful telescopes. ✉ *About 23 mi east of Grand Canyon Village on Desert View Dr.* ☎ *928/638-2736* ⊙ *Daily 8–7, hrs may vary.*

Grandview Point. At an elevation of 7,496 feet, the view from here is one of the finest in the canyon. To the northeast is a group of dominant buttes, including Krishna Shrine, Vishnu Temple, Rama Shrine, and Shiva Temple. A short stretch of the Colorado River is also visible. Directly below the point, and accessible by the steep and rugged Grandview Trail, is Horseshoe Mesa, where you can see the ruins of Last Chance Copper Mine. ✉ *About 12 mi east of Grand Canyon Village on Desert View Dr.*

★ **Hopi Point.** From this elevation of 7,071 feet, you can see a large section of the Colorado River; although it appears as a thin line, the river is nearly 350 feet wide below this overlook. The overlook extends farther into the canyon than any other point on Hermit Road. The unobstructed views make this a popular place to watch the sunset. Across the canyon to the north is Shiva Temple, which remained an isolated section of the Kaibab Plateau until 1937. That year, Harold Anthony of the American Museum of Natural History led an expedition to the rock formation in the belief that it supported life that had been cut off from the rest of the canyon. Imagine the expedition members' surprise when they found an empty Kodak film box on top of the temple. Directly below Hopi Point lies Dana Butte, named for a prominent 19th-century geologist. In 1919, an entrepreneur proposed connecting Hopi Point, Dana Butte, and the Tower of Set across the river with an aerial tramway, a technically feasible plan that fortunately has not been realized. ✉ *About 4 mi west of Hermit Road Junction on Hermit Rd.*

Hermits Rest. This westernmost viewpoint and Hermit Trail, which descends from it, were named for "hermit" Louis Boucher, a 19th-century French-Canadian prospector who had a number of mining claims and a roughly-built home down in the canyon. Views from here include Hermit

Desert View Drive

Desert View
see map below

64

**East
Entrance**

TO CAMERON →

Navajo Point
Lipan Point

Tusayn Ruin and Museum

Moran Point

Desert View Dr.

64

Grandview Point

Yaki Point

Desert View Dr.

Mather Point

Yavapai Point

Grand Canyon
Village

Park
Headquaters

Canyon View
Information
Plaza

South Entrance

64

Desert View Area

Watchtower

Bookstore/Information

Trading Post

Marketplace

Restrooms

Desert View
Campground

P

P

Service Station
(Seasonal)

**East
Entrance**

0   5 mi

0   5 km

Ten-X Campground

Grand Canyon Airport

Tusayan

↓ TO WILLIAMS,
FLAGSTAFF

64

Rapids and the towering cliffs of the Supai and Redwall formations. The stone building at Hermits Rest sells curios and refreshments. ⊠*About 8 mi west of Hermit Road Junction on Hermit Rd.*

Lipan Point. Here, at the canyon's widest point, you can get an astonishing visual profile of the gorge's geologic history, with a view of every eroded layer of the canyon. The spacious panorama stretches to the Vermilion Cliffs on the northeastern horizon and features a multitude of imaginatively named spires, buttes, and temples. You can also see Unkar Delta, where a creek joins the Colorado to form powerful rapids and a broad beach. Ancestral Puebloan farmers worked the Unkar Delta for hundreds of years, growing corn, beans, and melons. ⊠*About 25 mi east of Grand Canyon Village on Desert View Dr.*

Maricopa Point. This site merits a stop not only for the arresting scenery, which includes the Colorado River below, but also for its view of a defunct mine. On your left, as you face the canyon, are the Orphan Mine, a mine shaft, and cable lines leading up to the rim. The mine, which started operations in 1893, was worked first for copper and then for uranium until the venture came to a halt in 1969. The Battleship, the red butte directly ahead of you in the canyon, was named during the Spanish-American War, when battleships were in the news. ⊠*About 2 mi west of Hermit Road Junction on Hermit Rd.*

Mather Point. You'll likely get your first glimpse of the canyon from this viewpoint, one of the most impressive and accessible on the South Rim. Named for the National Park Service's first director, Stephen Tyng Mather, this spot yields extraordinary views of the Grand Canyon, including deep into the Inner Gorge and numerous buttes: Wotan's Throne, Brahma Temple, and Zoroaster Temple, among others. The Grand Canyon Lodge, on the North Rim, is almost directly north from Mather Point and only 10 mi away—yet you have to drive 215 mi to get from one spot to the other. ⊠*Near Canyon View Information Plaza.*

Mohave Point. Some of the canyon's most magnificent stone spires and buttes visible from this lesser-known overlook include the Tower of Set; the Tower of Ra; and Isis, Osiris, and Horus temples. From here you can also view the 5,401-foot Cheops Pyramid, a grayish-rock formation behind Dana Butte, plus some of the strongest rapids on the Colorado River. The Granite and Salt Creek rapids are

TRIP PLANNING

Before you go, request the complimentary *Trip Planner*, updated regularly by the National Park Service, by writing to: Trip Planner, Grand Canyon National Park, Box 129, Grand Canyon, AZ 86023. You can also get the trip planner online at ⊕ *www.nps.gov/ grca/grandcanyon/trip_planner.htm*. Several Web sites also are useful for trip-planning, including the National Park Service's Web site, www. nps.gov, as well as www. thecanyon.com, a commercial site with information on lodging, dining, and general park basics.

Once you arrive at the park, pick up *The Guide*, a free newspaper with a detailed area map and a schedule of free park programs. The park also distributes *The Grand Canyon Accessibility Guide*, also free, which can be picked up at visitor centers.

navigable, but not without plenty of effort. ⊠*About 5 mi west of Hermit Road Junction on Hermit Rd.*

Moran Point. This point was named for American landscape artist Thomas Moran, who was especially fond of the play of light and shadows from this location. He first visited the canyon with John Wesley Powell in 1873. "Thomas Moran's name, more than any other, with the possible exception of Major Powell's, is to be associated with the Grand Canyon," wrote noted canyon photographer Ellsworth Kolb. It's fitting that Moran Point is a favorite spot of photographers and painters. ⊠*About 17 mi east of Grand Canyon Village on Desert View Dr.*

Navajo Point. A possible site of the first Spanish view into the Canyon in 1540, this peak is also at the highest elevation (7,498 feet) on the South Rim. ⊠*About 21 mi east of Grand Canyon Village on Desert View Dr.*

Pima Point. Enjoy a bird's-eye view of Tonto Platform and Tonto Trail, which winds its way through the canyon for more than 70 mi. Also to the west, two dark, cone-shape mountains—Mount Trumbull and Mount Logan—are visible on the North Rim on clear days. They rise in stark contrast to the surrounding flat-top mesas and buttes. ⊠*About 7 mi west of Hermit Road Junction on Hermit Rd.*

Trailview Overlook. Look down on a dramatic view of the Bright Angel and Plateau Point trails as they zigzag down the canyon. In the deep gorge to the north flows Bright

Angel Creek, one of the region's few permanent tributary streams of the Colorado River. Toward the south is an unobstructed view of the distant San Francisco Peaks, as well as Bill Williams Mountain (on the horizon) and Red Butte (about 15 mi south of the canyon rim). ⊠ *About 2 mi west of Hermit Road Junction on Hermit Rd.*

Yaki Point. Stop here for an exceptional view of Wotan's Throne, a flat-top butte named by François Matthes, a U.S. Geological Survey scientist who developed the first topographical map of the Grand Canyon. The overlook juts out over the canyon, providing unobstructed views of inner-canyon-rock formations, South Rim cliffs, and Clear Creek Canyon. This point marks the beginning of the South Kaibab Trail and is one of the best places on the South Rim to watch the sunset. ⊠ *2 mi east of Grand Canyon Village on Desert View Dr.*

★ **Yavapai Point.** The word Yavapai means "sun people" in Paiute, a group of nomadic Indians associated with the Grand Canyon. Appropriately, this is one of the best locations on the South Rim to watch the sunset as it illuminates the glorious grandeur below. Dominated by the Yavapai Observation Station, revamped in 2007, this point offers panoramic views of the mighty gorge through a wall of windows. Exhibits showcased here include videos of the canyon floor and the Colorado River, a scaled diorama of the canyon with National Park boundaries, fossils and rock fragments used to recreate the complex layers that make the canyon walls, and a display on the natural forces used to carve the chasm. Rangers dig even deeper into Grand Canyon geology with the free ranger program Geo Glimpse, offered twice daily. A guided afternoon nature walk completes the offerings. Check ahead for special-event and walk schedules. ⊠ *Adjacent to Grand Canyon Village* ⊠ *Free.*

RIDE THE RAILS

There is no need to deal with all of the other drivers racing to the South Rim. Forget the hassle of the twisting rim roads, jaywalking pedestrians, and jammed parking lots and sit back and relax in the comfy train cars of the Grand Canyon Railway. Live music and storytelling enliven the trip as you journey past the breathtaking landscape. The train departs from the depot every morning between 8:30 and 10:30 AM, depending on the season, and makes the 65-mi journey in 2¼ hours. You can do the round-trip in

Visionary Architect: Mary Colter

In an era dominated by men, Mary Elizabeth Jane Colter revolutionized architecture in the Southwest with her bold visions and pioneering philosophy. Colter worked with the Fred Harvey Company for more than 40 years, bringing her aesthetic sense of style to her distinctive projects. By incorporating essential pieces of the past into her buildings, she effectively blended structures into the landscape using natural materials at hand. Colter designed six structures at the Grand Canyon, her first project being the Hopi House. Completed in 1905, the multistory structure mimics the Hopi buildings in Old Oraibi, the oldest continually inhabited village in the United States.

Other influential buildings built under her direction at the South Rim include Hermits Rest (1914), a whimsical jumble of stones meant to resemble a mountain man's attempt at building a shelter; Lookout Studio (1914), a rustic studio built from native stone and log timbers; Phantom Ranch (1922), a group of primitive cabins at the bottom of the Grand Canyon; Desert View Watchtower (1932), a towering 70-foot structure modeled after the authentic ruins of Indian towers scattered throughout the Southwest; and Bright Angel Lodge (1935), built to blend with the 1890s pioneer buildings at Bright Angel Camp.

Bright Angel Lodge features a fireplace mimicking the geologic strata in the canyon walls. The bottom layer is pieced together from Vishnu Schist, basement rocks from the inner gorge. The stone structure continues upward through the Grand Canyon Supergroup, the Paleozoic layers, and finally tops off with Kaibab limestone. The outline of the famous 10-foot-high fireplace also follows the profile contours of the alternating slopes and cliffs of the canyon walls. In subsequent years, Bright Angel Lodge became the model for the early architecture in national parks.

a single day; however, you may choose to stay overnight at the South Rim and return to Williams the following afternoon.

GOOD READS. Books on many aspects of the canyon—geological, historical, and scenic—are for sale in the visitor centers, various gift shops, and museums at both rims, as well as through the **Grand Canyon Association** (✍ *Box 399, Grand Canyon 86023* ☎ *928/638-2481* ⊕ *www.grandcanyon.org*).

DAY HIKES

Although permits are not required for day hikes, you must have a backcountry permit for longer trips (⇨*Permits under Things to Consider in Grand Canyon Essentials at the end of this book*). Some of the more popular trails are listed in this chapter; more detailed information and maps can be obtained from the Backcountry Information Center. Also, rangers can help design a trip to suit your abilities.

Remember that the canyon has significant elevation changes and, in summer, extreme temperature ranges, which can pose problems for people who aren't in good shape or who have heart or respiratory problems. **Carry plenty of water and energy foods.** The majority of each year's 400 search-and-rescue incidents result from hikers underestimating the size of the canyon, hiking beyond their abilities, or not packing sufficient food and water.

Under no circumstances should you attempt a day hike from the rim to the river and back. Remember that when it's 80°F on the South Rim, it's 110°F on the canyon floor. Allow two to three days if you want to hike rim to rim (it's easier to descend from the North Rim, as it is more than 1,000 feet higher than the South Rim). ■TIP➔ If you are planning to hike into the canyon and stay overnight at Phantom Ranch or its campground, you may wish to take advantage of the Duffel Service offered by Xanterra. For $60.83 each way, you can have mules carry your heavy pack or duffel loaded with camping gear (up to 30 pounds) into and out of the canyon. The service is offered daily from March through December, weekdays only in January and February. For contact information, *see* ⇨ Mule Rides in Summer Sports & Activities, below.

SPOTLIGHT HIKE: BRIGHT ANGEL TRAIL

★ Well-maintained, this is one of the most scenic hiking paths from the South Rim to the bottom of the canyon (9.6 mi each way). Plateau Point, about 1½ mi below Indian Garden, is as far as you should attempt to go on a day hike. Bright Angel Trail is the easiest of all the footpaths into the canyon, but because the climb out from the bottom is an ascent of 5,510 feet, the trip should be attempted only by those in good physical condition and should be avoided in midsummer due to extreme heat. Originally a bighorn-sheep path and later used by the Havasupai, the trail was widened late in the 19th century for prospectors

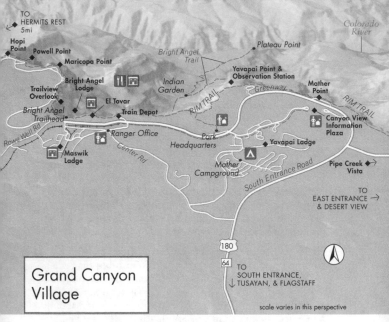

scale varies in this perspective

and is now used for both mule and foot traffic. ✉ *The trailhead is just west of Kolb Studio, Grand Canyon Village* ☞ *Moderate to difficult.*

1½ MI: MILE-AND-A-HALF REST HOUSE

The first section of the trail travels through Kaibab Formation, which is dotted with 270-million-year-old marine fossils. Keep an eye out for Indian pictographs in Mallery's Grotto, just after passing though the first tunnel. The second tunnel crosses the Bright Angel Fault, which extends for miles across the canyon. You'll find shade trees, seasonal water, and a compost toilet at Mile-and-a-Half Rest House, one of three resthouses on Bright Angel constructed by the Civilian Conservation Corps in 1935–1936.

3 MI: THREE-MILE REST HOUSE

The Redwall limestone cliffs below this rest house mark the dividing line between forest and desert habitats. Dramatic climate changes occur here. A spur takes hikers to a viewpoint overlooking Indian Garden and Plateau Point. From this point, the trail drops steeply down a series of switchbacks called Jacobs Ladder. This section of the trail

BRIGHT ANGEL TRAIL TIPS

- Hikers going downhill should yield to those going uphill.
- Mule trains have the right-of-way.
- If you are going on a day hike, you really shouldn't go beyond Indian Garden.
- It takes at least twice as long to go back up the trail as it does to come down.
- Rest houses are equipped with water at the 1½- and 3-mi points (but only from May through September) and at Indian Garden (4 mi) year-round. Water is also available at Bright Angel Campground, 9¼ mi below the trailhead, year-round but you should always bring some water with you.
- Emergency phones are located at Mile-and-a-Half, Three-Mile, and the River rest houses, as well as at Indian Garden and Bright Angel Campground.

can become extremely icy and slick in the winter, requiring the use of crampons.

4.6 MI: INDIAN GARDEN

Springs seep through the rocks at this popular stop on the trail. In the past, Havasupai Indians farmed this area seasonally. Today hikers will find a campground, ranger station, picnic tables, bathrooms, water, and the trailhead to Plateau Point. Plateau Point Trail, which is as far as you should go on a day hike, leads 1½ mi from Indian Garden across the Tonto Platform for impressive views of the inner canyon and the Colorado River.

7.7 MI: RIVER TRAIL JUNCTION

The next 3 mi descend down the Tapeats Narrows, a sandstone formation making up the lower strata on the Tonto Group, and past Garden Creek, a permanent water source used by Ancestral Puebloan Indians for irrigation. (Note: Rangers warn hikers to not drink untreated water from Garden Creek.) A set of switchbacks called the Devils Corkscrew traverse through Vishnu Schist, passing by streamside habitats and cliff springs. The River Rest House marks the River Trail junction, built by the Civilian Conservation Corps between 1933 and 1936. The River Trail connects the Bright Angel Trail to Phantom Ranch.

9.6 MI: PHANTOM RANCH

For the last leg of the trip, the trail follows along the Colorado River to the Silver Bridge, which is located below the mouth of Bright Angel Creek. Originally built in the late 1960s to support a pipeline transporting water from Roaring Spring on the North Rim to services on the South Rim, this suspension bridge is now used by hikers crossing the river to Bright Angel Campground and Phantom Ranch on the north side.

SPOTLIGHT HIKE: SOUTH KAIBAB TRAIL

This trail starts at Yaki Point on Desert View Drive, 4 mi east of Grand Canyon Village. Because the trail is so steep—descending from the trailhead at 7,260 feet down to 2,480 feet at the Colorado River—and has no water, many hikers return via the less-demanding Bright Angel Trail. During this 6.4-mi trek to the Colorado River, you're likely to encounter mule trains and riders. At the river, the trail crosses a suspension bridge and runs on to Phantom Ranch. Along the trail there is no water and very little shade. The trail corkscrews down through some spectacular geology. Look for (but don't remove) fossils in the limestone when taking water breaks. ⊠ *The trailhead at Yaki Point, 4 mi east of Grand Canyon Village* ☞ *Moderate to difficult.*

1 MI: OOH AAH POINT
South Kaibab Trail leaves the trailhead and immediately descends through a set of switchbacks called the Chimney. At Ooh Aah Point, 600 feet below the rim, the canyon opens up with panoramic views.

1½ MI: CEDAR RIDGE
Cedar Ridge is as far as you should go on a day hike in the summer months. There is no water, but there are portable toilets at this key point. Look for the fossil leaf impressions on the left (west) side of the ridge.

3 MI: SKELETON POINT
The next mile-and-a-half winds its way down from the Hermit formation to the Redwall Limestone at Skeleton Point at 2,040 feet. Great views open up to the west where you can see the dramatic grouping of Cheops Pyramid, Isis Temple, and Shiva Temple. To the east you can see Wotans Throne and Cape Royal. Day hikers should not travel past this point, even though the Colorado River and the Phantom Ranger Station are visible below. Continuing hikers should keep an eye out for trilobites and brachiopods as

SOUTH KAIBAB TRAIL TIPS

■ South Kaibab Trail offers the best views with the least amount of hiking; a trip to Ooh Aah Point, 600 feet below the rim, offers panoramic views.

■ In the summer months, avoid extreme midday temperatures by hiking early in the morning or late in the afternoon.

■ Mule trains have the right-of-way.

■ Water is only available at the trailhead.

■ This is the shortest route from the South Rim to Phantom Ranch, but due to the lack of shade and water rangers advise overnight hikers to ascend on Bright Angel Trail.

■ A Hiker's Express shuttle departs from Bright Angel Lodge and the Backcountry Information Office directly to the trailhead in September (5, 6, and 7 AM), October (6, 7, and 8 AM), and November (7, 8, and 9 AM)

the trail continues its descent through the Muav Limestone and Bright Angel Shale.

4.6 MI: THE TIPOFF

Toilets and an emergency phone are also available at the Tipoff, 4½ mi down the trail (3 mi past Cedar Ridge). Directly after this point, the trail plunges down 1,600 feet through Granite Gorge. At Panorama Point, ½ mi past the Tipoff, you can see the Kaibab Suspension and the Bright Angel Delta 1,200 feet below.

6.4 MI: KAIBAB SUSPENSION BRIDGE

After the River Trail junction, the South Kaibab Trail follows the last set of switchbacks and passes through a short tunnel before approaching the Kaibab Suspension Bridge. Built by the National Park Service in 1928, this bridge is also used by mule trains heading to and from Phantom Ranch, which is on the other side of the river. The North Kaibab Trail begins on the far side of the bridge.

OTHER HIKES

Boucher Trail. Named after prospector Louis Boucher, this rugged wilderness route follows a steep trail to Boucher Rapid on the Colorado River. Only for experienced canyon hikers, this 10½-mi, one-way trail begins at Hermit Trailhead and follows Dripping Springs trail to the junction at Boucher Trailhead. From Boucher Trailhead, the next 8 mi drop in a dramatic descent past Whites Butte and down Boucher Creek to the river. ✉ *Trail begins at Hermit Trailhead, 500 feet west of Hermit's Rest, approx. 8 mi west of Hermit Rd. Junction on Hermit Rd.* ☞ *Difficult.*

NEED A BREAK? If you've been driving too long and want some exercise, along with great views of the canyon, it's an easy 1¼-mi-long hike from the Information Plaza to El Tovar Hotel. The path runs through a quiet wooded area for about ½ mi, and then along the rim for another ¾ mi.

Grandview Trail. Accessible from the parking area at Grandview Point, the trailhead is at 7,400 feet. The path heads down 4.8 mi into the canyon to the junction and campsite at East Horseshoe Mesa Trail. Classified as a wilderness trail, the route is aggressive and not as heavily traveled as some of the more well-known trails, such as Bright Angel and Hermit; allow six to nine hours, round-trip. There is no water available along the trail, which follows a steep descent to 4,800 feet at Horseshoe Mesa, where Hopi Indians once collected mineral paints. ✉ *Trail at Grandview Point, approx. 12 mi east of Grand Canyon Village on Desert View Dr.* ☞ *Difficult.*

Hermit Trail. Beginning on the South Rim just west of Hermits Rest (and 8 mi west of Grand Canyon Village), this steep, 9.3-mi (one-way) trail drops more than 5,000 feet to Hermit Creek, which usually flows year-round. It's a strenuous hike back up and is recommended for experienced long-distance hikers only; plan for six to nine hours. There's an abundance of lush growth and wildlife, including desert bighorn sheep, along this trail.

The trail descends from the trailhead at 6,640 feet to the Colorado River at 2,400 feet. Day hikers should not go past Santa Maria Springs at 4,880 feet. For much of the year, no water is available along the way; ask a park ranger about the availability of water at Santa Maria Springs and Hermit Creek before you set out. All water from these sources should be treated before drinking. The route leads down to the Colorado River and has inspiring views of Hermit Gorge and Redwall and Supai formations. Six miles from the trailhead are the ruins of Hermit Camp, which the Santa Fe Railroad ran as a tourist camp from 1911 until 1930. ✉ *Trail begins at Hermit Trailhead, 500 feet west of Hermit's Rest, approx. 8 mi west of Hermit Rd. Junction on Hermit Rd.* ☞ *Difficult.*

New Hance Trail. One of the most difficult, but also one of the most scenic, the New Hance Trail qualifies as a wilderness route and should only be attempted by experienced canyon hikers. To reach the trailhead, park at Moran Point and walk 1 mi south along the rim to the trailhead. The rugged route, named after famous canyon guide John Hance, follows steep switchbacks through Red Canyon before ending at Hance Rapids on the Colorado River, just above the head of Granite Gorge. ⊠ *Trailhead 1 mi south of Moran Point, which is approx. 17 mi east of Grand Canyon Village on Desert View Dr.* ☞ *Very difficult.*

★ **Fodor's Choice Rim Trail.** The South Rim's most popular walking path is the 9-mi (one-way) Rim Trail, which runs along the edge of the canyon from Mather Point (the first overlook on Desert View Drive) to Hermits Rest. This walk, which is paved to Maricopa Point, visits several of the South Rim's historic landmarks. Allow anywhere from 15 minutes to a full day; the Rim Trail is an ideal day hike, as it varies only a few hundred feet in elevation from Mather Point (7,120 feet) to the trailhead at Hermits Rest (6,640 feet). The trail also can be accessed from the major viewpoints along Hermit Road, which are serviced by shuttle buses during the busy summer months. ⊠ *Trail runs from Mather Point, near Canyon View Information Plaza, to Hermit's Rest, approx. 8 mi west of Hermit Rd. Junction on Hermit Rd.* ☞ *Easy.*

South Bass Trail. Once used as an Indian footpath, this trail was improved by canyon pioneer William Bass. The trail descends down steep switchbacks, past a prehistoric granary, through a redbud-tree grove, across the Tonto Platform, and down to Bass Rapid on the Colorado River. ⊠ *Trailhead off Forest Service Rd. 328, 31 mi west of Grand Canyon Village* ☞ *Difficult.*

Tanner Trail. Following a prehistoric Indian footpath, this wilderness route begins just east of Lipan Point and follows a series of steep switchbacks through the Supai Group, winds around the base of Escalante and Cardenas Buttes, and continues to descend down Tanner Canyon to the Colorado River. ⊠ *Trailhead east of Lipan Point, which is approx. 25 mi east of Grand Canyon Village on Desert View Dr.* ☞ *Difficult.*

Tonto Trail. Stretching 95 mi from Garnet Canyon to Red Canyon along the Tonto Platform, this trail is predominately used to connect rim to river routes, especially along

the 4½-mi section traversing from Bright Angel Trail to the South Kaibab Trail. While appearing level, the Tonto Trail actually travels up and down various drainage routes which connect to the Colorado River, and varies elevations at 3,600 feet at Red Canyon to 2,800 feet at Garnet Canyon. Approximate distances from major connecting points include Hermit Creek to Indian Garden on the Bright Angel Trail (12 mi), South Kaibab Trail to Horseshoe Mesa on the Grandview Trail (21 mi), and Horseshoe Mesa and the Grandview Trail to the New Hance Trail (10 mi). ⊠ *Links many trails in the Lower Canyon area* ⌖ *Difficult.*

SUMMER SPORTS & ACTIVITIES

AIR TOURS

★ Flights by plane and helicopter over the canyon are offered by a number of companies, departing for the Grand Canyon Airport at the south end of Tusayan. Prices and lengths of tours vary, but you can expect to pay about $109 to $120 per adult for plane trips and approximately $130 to $235 for helicopter tours.

OUTFITTERS & EXPEDITIONS

Companies worth noting are **Air Grand Canyon** (⊠*Grand Canyon Airport, Tusayan* ☎*928/638–2686 or 800/247–4726* ⊕*www.airgrandcanyon.com*), **Grand Canyon Airlines** (⊠*Grand Canyon Airport, Tusayan* ☎*928/638–2359 or 866/235–9422* ⊕*www.grandcanyonairlines.com*), **Grand Canyon Helicopters** (⊠*Grand Canyon Airport, Tusayan* ☎*928/638–2764 or 800/541–4537* ⊕*www.grandcanyon helicoptersaz.com*), **Maverick Helicopters** (⊠*Grand Canyon Airport, Tusayan* ☎*928/638–2622 or 800/962–3869* ⊕*www.maverickhelicopters.com*), and **Papillon Grand Canyon Helicopters** (⊠*Grand Canyon Airport, Tusayan* ☎*928/638–2419 or 800/528–2418* ⊕*www.papillon.com*).

BICYCLING

Narrow shoulders on park roads and heavy traffic limit off-road-biking opportunities in the South Rim, which may disappoint hard-core cyclists. Bicycles are permitted on all park roads and on the multiuse Greenway System, currently under development. Bikes are prohibited on all

HIKING

	Grade	Miles (one-way)	Beginning Elevation (feet)	Ending Elevation (feet)	Mules	Campground	Open Info	Water	Shuttle Access	Range Station	Toilet/Restroom	Emergency Telephone	Level	Conditions
Boucher Trail	Very Steep	10.5	6640	2760	N	N	Y/R	Y**	Y	N	Y*	N	Diff.	Unmaintained
Bright Angel Trail South	Steep	9.3	6860	2480	Y	Y	Y/R	Y*	Y	Y	Y	Y	Mod.	Maintained
Grandview Trail	Very Steep	3.2	7400	4800	N	Y	Y/R	N	Y	N	Y**	Y**	Diff.	Unmaintained
Hermit Trail	Steep	9.3	6640	2400	N	Y	Y/R	Y	Y	N	Y**	Y**	Diff.	Unmaintained
New Hance Trail	Steep	8	7000	2600	N		Y/R	Y	Y	Y	Y	Y	Diff.	Unmaintained
Rim Trail	Level	9	6640	7120	N	N	Y/R	Y	Y		Y	Y	Easy	Maintained
South Bass Trail	Steep	7.8	6650	2250	N	Y	Y/R	Y**	N	N	N	N	Diff.	Unmaintained
South Kaibab Trail	Steep	7.1	7260	2546	Y	N	Y/R	Y**	Y	Y	Y	Y	Mod.	Maintained
Tanner Trail	Very Steep	10	7300	2700	N	N	Y/R	Y	N	N	N	N	Diff.	Unmaintained

* Water is seasonal   ** at trailhead only   Y/R = year-round   M = Maintained   U = Unmaintained

FLYING TO THE CANYON

Several carriers fly to the Grand Canyon Airport from Las Vegas, including **Air Vegas** (☎ *800/940-2550* ⊕ *www.airvegas.com*), **Scenic Airlines** (☎ *800/634-6801* ⊕ *www.scenic.com*), and **Vision Holidays** (☎ *800/256-8767* ⊕ *www.visionholidays.com*). North Las Vegas Airport is the primary air hub for flights to Grand Canyon National Parks Airport. You can also make connections into the Grand Canyon from Phoenix Sky Harbor International Airport (PHX).

Xanterra Transportation Company (☎ *928/638-2822*) offers 24-hour taxi service at Grand Canyon Airport, Grand Canyon Village, and the nearby village of Tusayan. Taxis also make trips to other destinations in and around Grand Canyon National Park.

other trails, including the Rim Trail. Mountain bikers visiting the South Rim may be better off meandering through the ponderosa-pine forest on the Tusayan Bike Trail. No rentals are available at the canyon.

HORSEBACK RIDING

Get back to nature and away from the rim's pressing crowds with a horseback ride through the forest. Another option is to bring your own stock (horses, mules, donkeys, and burros). Private livestock is limited to the corridor trails (Bright Angel Trail and South Kaibab Trail) in the inner canyon and on select rim trails. Bright Angel and Cottonwood campgrounds accommodate private equines, as does the South Rim Horse Camp, located a ½ mi from the Bright Angel Trailhead. Grazing is not permitted; handlers are required to pack their own feed.

OUTFITTERS & EXPEDITIONS

Apache Stables. There's nothing like a horseback ride to immerse you in the Western experience. From stables behind the Moqui Lodge near Tusayan, these folks offer gentle horses and a ride that will meet most budgets. Choose from one- and two-hour trail rides or the popular campfire rides and horse-drawn wagon excursions. ⊠ *Forest Service Rd. 328, 1 mi north of Tusayan* ☎ *928/638-3105* ⊕ *www.apachestables.com* ⊠ *$25.50–$85.50* ☉ *Mar.–Nov., daily; call ahead for hrs.*

Backcountry Information Center. Backcountry permits are required for overnight horseback-riding trips and for overnight use of the South Rim Horse Camp. To increase your chances for obtaining a permit, make your request as early as possible. Reservations are taken up to four months in advance. Contact Grand Canyon National Park's Backcountry Information Center for a copy of the *Backcountry Trip Planner.* ⊕*Box 129, Grand Canyon 86023* ☎*928/638–7875* ⊟*928/638–2125* ⊕*www.nps.gov/grca* ⊠*$5 per stock animal per night* ⊟*AE, D, MC, V* ⚲*Reservations essential.*

JEEP TOURS

Escape the crowds and take an off-road adventure off the beaten path with jeep tour of the South Rim. ■TIP➔ **Rides can be rough; if you have had back injuries, check with your doctor before taking a jeep tour.**

OUTFITTERS & EXPEDITIONS
Grand Canyon Jeep Tours & Safaris. If you'd like to get off the pavement and see parts of the park that are accessible only by dirt road, a Jeep tour can be just the ticket. From March through October, Grand Jeep Tours & Safaris leads daily, 1½- to 4½-hour, off-road tours within the park, as well as in Kaibab National Forest. Combo tours adding helicopter and airplane rides are available. ⊕*Box 1772, Grand Canyon 86023* ☎*928/638–5337 or 800/320–5337* ⊕*www.grandcanyonjeeptours.com* ⊠*$45–$209* ⊟*AE, MC, V* ⚲*Reservations essential.*

Grand Canyon Old West Jeep Tours. This tour company offers off-road jeep adventures and backcountry ATV adventures for visitors looking to explore the South Rim off the beaten path. From March through November, Grand Canyon Old West Jeep Tours offers two- and three-hour, off-road and helicopter/jeep combo tours of the South Rim. The all-day trip to the inner canyon on the Hualapai Indian reservation is offered year-round. ⊠*Grand Canyon* ☎*928/638–2000 or 866/638–4386* ⊕*www.grandcanyonjeeps.com* ⊠*$63–$256* ⊟*AE, D, MC, V* ⚲*Reservations essential.*

Marvelous Marv's Grand Canyon Tour. For a personalized experience, take this private tour of the Grand Canyon and surrounding sights any time of year. Tours include round-trip transportation from your hotel or campground in Williams, Tusayan, or Grand Canyon; admission to the park;

scenic viewpoint stops; a short hike; and personal narra-
tion of the geology and history of the area. ⊡)*Box 544,
Williams 86046* ☎*928/707–0291* ⊕*www.marvelousmarv.
com* ✉*$85* ⊟*No credit cards* ⚠*Reservations essential.*

MULE RIDES

★ Mule rides provide an intimate glimpse into the canyon
for those who have the time but not the stamina to see the
canyon on foot. Reservations are essential and are accepted
up to 23 months in advance, or you can check the waiting
list for last-minute cancellations.

These trips have been conducted since the early 1900s. A
comforting fact as you ride the narrow trail: No one's ever
been killed while riding a mule that fell off a cliff. (Nevertheless, the treks are not for the faint of heart or people in
questionable health.)

ARRANGING TOURS

Transportation-services desks are maintained at El Tovar,
Bright Angel, Maswik Lodge, and Yavapai Lodge (closed
in winter) in Grand Canyon Village. The desks provide
information and handle bookings for sightseeing tours, taxi
and bus services, mule and horseback rides, and accommodations at Phantom Ranch (at the bottom of the Grand
Canyon). The concierge at El Tovar can also arrange most
tours, with the exception of mule rides and lodging at
Phantom Ranch. On the North Rim, Grand Canyon Lodge
has general information about local services.

Hikers can also take advantage of the mules by paying to
have their heavy packs or duffels carried down into the
canyon. You must pay each way, and the weight limit is 30
pounds. The service is offered daily from March through
December, weekdays only in January and February. The
service must be reserved and paid for in advance, but you
can usually do this after you arrive at the canyon.

OUTFITTERS

Grand Canyon National Park Lodges Mule Rides. These trips
delve into the canyon from the South Rim. Riders must be
at least 4-feet, 7-inches tall, weigh less than 200 pounds,
and understand English. Children under 15 must be accompanied by an adult. Riders must be in fairly good physical
condition; pregnant women are advised not to take these
trips. The all-day ride to Plateau Point costs $153.95 (box

lunch included). An overnight with a stay at Phantom
Ranch at the bottom of the canyon is $420.09 ($743.03
for two riders). Two nights at Phantom Ranch, an option
available from November through March, will set you
back $592.83 ($991.38 for two). Meals are included. Reservations, especially during the busy summer months are a
must (and can be made up to two years in advance), but
you can check at the Bright Angel Transportation Desk to
be placed on the waiting list. Winter reservations (December through February) are much less of a problem and can
often be obtained at the last minute. *6312 S. Fiddlers
Green Circle, Ste. 600N, Greenwood Village, CO 80111*
☎*303/297–2757 or 888/297–2757* ☎*303/297–3175*
⊕*www.grandcanyonlodges.com* ☉ *Daily; call ahead for
departures.*

RAFTING

You don't have to take a multiday white-water excursion
to see the canyon from the Colorado River. The popular
15½-mi smooth-water-float trip begins at the base of Glen
Canyon Dam and ends at Lees Ferry. Allow a full day for
this trip. Prices, which include lunch, range from $118 to
$141.

OUTFITTERS & EXPEDITIONS
Companies to contact on the South Rim include **Grand Canyon Airlines** (⊠*Grand Canyon Airport, Tusayan* ☎*928/638–
2359 or 866/235–9422* ⊕*www.grandcanyonairlines.com*)
and **Grand Canyon Helicopters** (⊠*Grand Canyon Airport,
Tusayan* ☎*928/638–2764 or 800/541–4537* ⊕*www.
grandcanyonhelicoptersaz.com*).

SIGHTSEEING TOURS

Beat the crowds with a guided tour of South Rim sights.

OUTFITTERS & EXPEDITIONS
American Dream Tours. All-day tours include wildlife viewing, visits to Indian ruins and abandoned mines, and scenic
South Rim views, as well as pick-up from Flagstaff, Williams, Tusayan, and Grand Canyon Village. Fees include
round-trip transportation, entrance fees, and a picnic
lunch. Save $10 by booking online. *Box 2822, Flagstaff
86004* ☎*888/203–1212* ⊕*www.americandreamtours.com*
☎*$98* ⊟*AE, D, MC, V* ⚲*Reservations essential.*

Angel's Gate Tours. Naturalists take visitors on an all-day excursion to South Rim overlooks, fossil beds, and Indian petroglyphs and ruins. Day hikes, ranging from family-friendly "mild" hikes to rugged "extreme" hikes, are also offered. Fees include entry, lunch, and hotel pickup. *112 Kletha Trail, Flagstaff 86001 928/814–2277 or 800/957–4557 www.grandcanyonjeeptours.com $109–$245 AE, D, MC, V Reservations essential.*

Discover Grand Canyon. Located on the South Rim, this local tour operator offers morning and evening tours of the South Rim. *Box 3398, Grand Canyon 86023 928/638–1088 www.discovergrandcanyontours.com $60–$75 AE, D, MC, V Reservations essential.*

WINTER SPORTS & ACTIVITIES

SKIING

Although you can't schuss down into the Grand Canyon, you can cross-country ski in the woods near the rim when there's enough snow. The best time for cross-country skiing is mid-December though early March. Trails, suitable for beginner and intermediate skiers, begin 0.3 mi north of the Grandview Lookout and travel through the Kaibab National Forest. Contact the **Tusayan Ranger District** (*Box 3088, Grand Canyon 86023 928/638–2443 www. fs.fed.us/r3/kai*) for details.

EXPLORING THE BACKCOUNTRY

Of the 4.5 million people traveling to Grand Canyon National Park each year, only a small fraction spend more than a day exploring the rim and even fewer actually explore its secrets on an overnight trip into its depths. The park encompasses more than 1.2 million acres, but only a small portion of this rugged countryside can be accessed by hikers. Each year more than 30,000 overnight-permit requests flood the Backcountry Information Center but, only 13,000 permits are issued. Due to the fragile desert environment and careful monitoring by the park service, the demand usually exceeds permit availability. The Colorado River separates the South Rim and the North Rim, with the only river crossing at Phantom Ranch. The best seasons to hike the canyon are spring and fall, but are also the most difficult times to obtain a permit. Be sure to allow twice as much time to ascend the canyon as to hike down. Rangers suggest a minimum of one or two nights for a round-trip hike from the South Rim to the Colorado River.

BACKCOUNTRY INFORMATION CENTER

Backcountry Information Center. Backcountry permits are required for all overnight stays including overnight hiking, overnight horseback riding, overnight cross-country ski trips, and overnight camping at rim sites other than developed campgrounds. To increase your chances for obtaining a permit, make your request as early as possible. Reservations can be made up to four months in advance. Contact Grand Canyon National Park's Backcountry Information Center for a copy of the *Backcountry Trip Planner.* ⊕*Box 129, Grand Canyon 86023* ☎*928/638–7875* 🖷*928/638–2125* ⊕*www.nps.gov/grca* ✉*$10 per permit plus $5 per person, per night* ⊟*AE, D, MC, V* ⚓*Reservations essential.*

EDUCATIONAL PROGRAMS

Discover the flora and fauna of the Grand Canyon, explore prehistoric life along exposed fossil beds, take an interpretive guided hike, and uncover the layered geologic history of the canyon with educational tours and scheduled ranger programs.

GRAND CANYON FIELD INSTITUTE

Grand Canyon Field Institute. Instructors lead guided educational tours, hikes around and into the canyon, and weekend programs at the South Rim. Tour topics include everything from archaeology and backcountry medicine to photography and natural history. Contact GCFI for a schedule and price list. ⊕*Box 399, Grand Canyon 86023* ☎*928/638–2485 or 866/471–4435* 🖷*928/638–2484* ⊕*www.grandcanyon.org/fieldinstitute* ✉*$115–$895* ⊟*AE, D, MC, V* ⚓*Reservations essential.*

Freebies at the Canyon

While you're here, be sure to take advantage of the many freebies offered at Grand Canyon National Park. The most useful of these services is the system of free shuttle buses at the South Rim; it caters to the road-weary, with three routes winding through the park—Hermits Rest Route, Village Route, and Kaibab Trail Route. Of the bus routes, the Hermits Rest Route runs only from March through November; the other two run year-round, and the Kaibab Trail Route provides the only access to Yaki Point. Hikers coming or going from the Kaibab Trailhead can catch the Hikers Express, which departs three times each morning from the Bright Angel Lodge, makes a quick stop at the Backcountry Office, and then heads out to the South Kaibab Trailhead.

Ranger-led programs are always free and offered year-round, though more are scheduled during the busy spring and summer seasons. These programs might include activities such as stargazing and topics such as geology and the cultural history of prehistoric peoples. Some of the more in-depth programs may include a fossil walk or a condor talk. Check with the visitor center for seasonal programs including wildflower walks and fire ecology.

Kids ages 4 to 14 can get involved with the park's Junior Ranger program, with ever-changing activities including hikes and hands-on experiments.

Despite all of these options, rangers will tell you that the best free activity in the canyon is watching the magnificent splashes of color on the canyon walls during sunrise and sunset.

RANGER PROGRAMS

☼ **Fossil Walk: Remnant Impressions.** The ½-mi, one-way walk explores an exposed fossil bed along the rim, where you'll see the remains of brachiopods, sponges, and other marine creatures. Walk departs from the patio of Bright Angel Lodge; allow 60 minutes. ☎928/638–7888 ⊕www.nps.gov/grca/forkids/index.htm ☝Free.

Interpretive Ranger Programs. The National Park Service sponsors all sorts of orientation activities, such as daily guided hikes and talks, at both the North and South rims. The focus may be on any aspect of the canyon—from geology and flora and fauna to history and early inhabitants. For schedules on the South Rim, go to Canyon View Information Plaza, pick up a free copy of *The Guide* to the South Rim, or check online. ☎*928/638–7888* ⊕*www.nps. gov/grca* ☞*Free.*

Introduction to Grand Canyon's Geology. Take an in-depth look at the creation and composition of the world's greatest gorge. Meet a park ranger at the Canyon View Information Plaza's Visitor Center; allow 45 minutes. ☎*928/638–7888* ⊕*www.nps.gov/grca* ☞*Free.*

☾ **Junior Ranger Program for Families.** Children ages 4 to 14 can take part in these hands-on educational programs. ☎*928/638–7888* ⊕*www.nps.gov/grca/forkids/index.htm* ☞*Free* ☉ *Year-round.*

☾ **Nature Walk.** Take a short hike along the rim and learn about animals and plants living within the boundaries of the Grand Canyon National Park. Topics may include rare and endangered species, nature's influence on writers and artists, Native American use of plants and animals, human impact on fragile ecologies, and seasonal adaptations made by indigenous plants and animals. Meet a park ranger outside the Yavapai Observation Station; allow 60 minutes. ☎*928/638–7888* ⊕*www.nps.gov/grca* ☞*Free.*

☾ **Way Cool for Kids.** Rangers coordinate these free, hour-long introductions to the park for children ages 7 to 11, daily at 9 AM. Kids and rangers walk around the Village Rim area and talk about local plants and animals, history, or archaeology. Programs are subject to change. ⊠*South Rim Park Headquarters, Parking Lot A* ☎*928/638–7888* ☞*Free.*

BRINGING YOUR PET. Pets are allowed in Grand Canyon National Park; however, they must be on a leash at all times. With the exception of service animals, pets are not allowed below the rim or on park shuttles. A **kennel** (☎*928/638–0534*), near the Maswik Lodge, houses cats and dogs. It is open daily from 7:30 to 5. Reservations are strongly recommended. To take a service animal below the rim, check in with the Backcountry Information Center, which is located in the Maswik Transportation Center.

CLOSE UP

Park Insider: Chuck Wahler

When Chuck Wahler tells people to "take a hike," he means it in the most helpful, encouraging sense. An 18-year employee at Grand Canyon National Park, Wahler knows the lay of the land, and he encourages folks to get a feel for it on foot. A hike "either along the rim or into the canyon" ranks among his top "must-do" suggestions for park visitors.

As Chief of the Operations Branch for the park's Division of Interpretation and Resource Education, Wahler manages front-line operations for the division. "The staff that works with me operates the park visitor centers and museums, and presents interpretive programs to our visitors," he explains.

Those programs include the popular "Junior Ranger" activities, which also make Wahler's must-do list: "If there are children in your group, have them participate."

Variety is the spice of park life, as far as Wahler is concerned, and the range of activities is his favorite thing about his workplace. "It is a constantly changing place," he says, "different from minute to minute, day to day, and season to season." That diversity inspires another suggestion: "Views of the canyon from along Hermit Road are very different from

those along Desert View Drive," explains Wahler. "If you have the time, plan to experience both areas of the park."

Navigating the 1,904-square-mi park is a sizeable task, but it's made easier by the free shuttle system. The buses stop at 30-some points of interest, and Wahler advocates hopping aboard whenever possible. "You'll spend more of your time exploring the park and less time looking for a place to park."

For another insider tip, he touts the park's aptly named newspaper. *The Guide* provides visitors with all the basic information they need to plan their visit to the park. Taking a few minutes to read the newspaper will help make a visit more enjoyable." Distributed at the entrance station, *The Guide* is printed in English, French, German, Spanish, Japanese, and Italian.

Wahler also urges travelers to consider coming during "the off-season" (late fall through early spring). "The weather can delightful, and the park is often less crowded than in the summer."

No matter the season, Wahler's final must-do is a simple one: "Find a quiet place along the rim, and just sit and enjoy the canyon."

2

BUS TOURS

Xanterra Motorcoach Tours. Narrated by knowledgeable guides, tours include the Hermits Rest Tour, which travels along the old wagon road built by the Santa Fe Railway; the Desert View Tour, which glimpses the Colorado River's rapids and stops at Lipan Point; and Sunrise and Sunset Tours. *6312 S. Fiddlers Green Circle, Ste. 600N, Greenwood Village, CO 80111* *303/297–2757 or 888/297–2757* *www.grandcanyonlodges.com* *$16 to $45 per person; children 16 and younger free when accompanied by a paying adult.*

ARTS & ENTERTAINMENT

Bright Angel Lounge (*Bright Angel Lodge, Grand Canyon Village* *928/638–2631*) is a casual lounge with a wide range of beverages and a limited menu. Murals brighten up the otherwise dark room and live entertainment jazzes up the busy weekend evenings with a variety of Western and folk music. Open year-round, 11 AM to 11 PM.

Rustic, yet elegant, **El Tovar Lounge** (*El Tovar Hotel, Grand Canyon Village* *928/638–2631*) offers stunning canyon views from the veranda and a nice selection of cocktails and appetizers. Open year-round, 11 AM to 11 PM.

End your day with a one-hour **Evening Program** (*928/638–7610* *www.nps.gov/grca*)on the canyon's natural or cultural history. The outdoor presentations are held daily at 7:30 PM at the Mather Amphitheater, located behind the park headquarters off the Rim Trail. Dress warmly and bring a flashlight. From October through April, the program moves inside to the Shrine of Ages Auditorium.

Full Moon Walks and Star Talks (*928/638–7888* *www.nps.gov/grca*) are held during the nights directly before, during, and after the full and new moon. Park rangers offer this special program one hour after sunset at Mather Point.

Stop by the laid-back **Maswik Sports Bar** (*Maswik Lodge, Grand Canyon Village* *928/638–2631*) to catch the latest sporting event, shoot a game of pool, or enjoy one of the many select draft beers or specialty drinks on the bar menu. The bar is open weekdays, from 5 to 11 PM, and weekends from 3 to 11 PM.

FESTIVALS & EVENTS

The **Community Lecture Series** (☏*800/858–2808* ⊕*www. grandcanyon.org*) offers two lectures each month on the natural and cultural history of the Grand Canyon and the Colorado Plateau.

★ The **Grand Canyon Music Festival** (☏*928/638–9215 or 800/997–8285* ⊕*www.grandcanyonmusicfest.org*) is held each September at the Shrine of Ages amphitheater and stages nearly a dozen concerts. In the early 1980s, music aficionados Robert Bonfiglio and Clare Hoffman hiked through the Grand Canyon and decided the stunning spectacle should be accompanied by the strains of a symphony. One of the park rangers agreed, and the wandering musicians performed an impromptu concert. Encouraged by the experience, Bonfiglio and Hoffman started the Grand Canyon Music Festival. Concerts are held on three consecutive weekends.

For an artistic look at the Grand Canyon, check out the changing exhibits at **Kolb Studio** (☏*800/858–2808* ⊕*www. grandcanyon.org/kolb*). Since 1993, the studio has hosted a series of Grand Canyon–oriented exhibits including "I Am the Grand Canyon," an introspective look at the canyon's Havasu Indians; "Lasting Light: 125 Years of Grand Canyon," an in-depth look at the change of light above and below the rim; and the annual "Legacies: Arts for Our Parks," an artistic showcase of works composed by students at the Grand Canyon School held each March in honor of National Youth Art Month.

Park rangers join representatives from HawkWatch International for the annual **Raptors in Flight** program (☏*928/ 638–7888* ⊕*www.nps.gov/grca* ✉*Free*). The ranger-led program is held twice daily at Yaki Point, where participating visitors learn to identify migrating raptors. HawkWatch representatives record the fall hawk migration at Lipan Point and Yaki Point daily from 10 to 4. Visitors are encouraged to join the count, which runs in September and October. For the Raptors in Flight program, meet a park ranger at Yaki Point; call ahead to confirm times and allow 45 minutes.

SHOPPING

Nearly every lodging facility and retail store at the South Rim stocks Native American arts and crafts and Grand Canyon books and souvenirs. Prices are comparable to other souvenir outlets, though you may find some better deals in Williams. However, a portion of the proceeds from items purchased at Hopi House, Desert Watchtower, and the visitor center go to the Grand Canyon Association. **Canyon Village Marketplace** sells groceries, but prices will be cheaper in Flagstaff, Williams, or Tusayan.

Bright Angel Gift Shop (⊠ *Desert View Rim Dr., Grand Canyon Village* ☏ *928/638–2631*) carries Native American pottery, T-shirts, and souvenirs.

Desert View Trading Post (⊠ *Desert View Dr., near the Watchtower at Desert View, Grand Canyon* ☏ *928/638–2360*) sells a mix of traditional Southwestern souvenirs and authentic Native American arts and crafts.

El Tovar Hotel Gift Shop (⊠ *Desert View Dr., Grand Canyon Village* ☏ *928/638–2631*) carries Native American jewelry, rather expensive casual wear, and souvenirs.

★ **Hopi House** (⊠ *Desert View Dr., east of El Tovar Hotel, Grand Canyon Village* ☏ *928/638–2631*) has the widest selection of Native American handicrafts in the vicinity.

Verkamp's Curios (⊠ *Desert View Dr., across from El Tovar Hotel, Grand Canyon Village* ☏ *928/638–2242 or 888/817–0806* ⊕ *www.verkamps.com*) is the best place on the South Rim to buy inexpensive souvenirs of your Grand Canyon adventure.

Exploring the North Rim

WORD OF MOUTH

"Of all the parks, I'd say [sitting on] the veranda at the Grand Canyon [Lodge] was the most relaxed way of either enjoying solitude or striking up a conversation. And then there's the view."

—carolv

By Carrie
Miner

AUTHOR EDWARD ABBEY ONCE WROTE: "I find that in contemplating the natural world my pleasure is greater if there are not too many others contemplating it with me, at the same time." The North Rim will give you that opportunity. Although it draws only about 10% of the Grand Canyon's visitors, many believe it is more gorgeous than the South Rim, and because of its remote location, it provides a more intimate and unhurried experience.

Although the North Rim is just 10 mi across from the South Rim, getting there by car is a 5-hour, 215-mi drive. At first it might not sound like the trip would be worth it, but the payoff is huge: those who make the North Rim trip often insist it offers the canyon's most beautiful views and best hiking. At 1,000 feet higher than the South Rim, the northern edge offers more expansive vistas of the buttes and ridges scattered through the wide expanse cut by the Colorado River millions of years ago. It's these long distances and lack of amenities that keep the North Rim and the surrounding Kaibab National Forest a pristine wonderland perfect for outdoor enthusiasts looking to explore shaded forests, broad meadows, and hidden waterways.

The Paiute word Kaibab means "mountain lying down," and this 9,000-foot-tall limestone plateau is just that—one of the highest points on the vast Colorado Plateau. The road to these alpine uplands rises out of the surrounding desert to an isolated forest stretching along the upper reaches of the Grand Canyon. Wildlife abounds in the thick ponderosa-pine forests and lush mountain meadows. It's common to see deer, turkeys, and coyotes as you drive through this remote region.

WHAT TO SEE

The North Rim's 8,000-foot elevation, which keeps things cool in summer, makes for an arduous winter, and the road to the North Rim closes from around mid-October through mid-May because of heavy snow. However, in summer months and early fall outdoor adventure rules. Lodgings are available but extremely limited; the North Rim only offers one historic lodge and restaurant and a single campground. Your best bet may be to pack your camping gear and hiking boots and take several days to explore the lush Kaibab Forest. This high-altitude playground is perfect for biking through the forest, sleeping under the stars, hik-

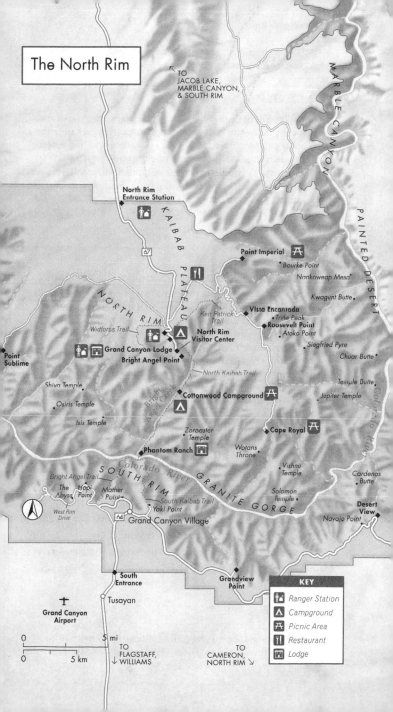

ing down hair-raising trails, bird-watching in old-growth
spruce, and communing with the canyon.

VISITOR CENTER

North Rim Visitor Center. View exhibits, peruse the bookstore,
and pick up useful maps and brochures. Rangers take the
time to chat with visitors while interactive exhibits entertain the younger set. Interpretive programs on a variety of
subjects are scheduled throughout the summer. If you're
craving coffee, it's a short walk from here to the Coffee
Salon in the Grand Canyon Lodge. ⊠*Near the parking lot
on Bright Angel Peninsula* ☎*928/638–7888* ⊙*Mid-May–
mid-Oct., daily 8–6.*

SCENIC DRIVE

★ **Highway 67.** Open mid-May to mid-October (and often
until Thanksgiving), the two-lane-paved road climbs 1,400
feet in elevation as it passes through the Kaibab National
Forest. Also called the "North Rim Parkway," this scenic
route crosses the limestone-capped Kaibab Plateau—passing broad meadows, sun-dappled forests, and small lakes
and springs—before abruptly falling away at the abyss of
the Grand Canyon. Point Imperial and Cape Royal can be
reached by spurs off this scenic drive running from Jacob
Lake to Bright Angel Point.

EN ROUTE. Unpaved forested side roads branch off of Highway 67
before the North Rim park-entrance station, leading to several
remote viewpoints not seen by the majority of Grand Canyon
travelers. At Crazy Jug Point, you'll see the Colorado River as
well as several canyon landmarks, including Powell Plateau,
Great Thumb Mesa, and Tapeats Amphitheater. Timp Point
features spectacular canyon views and a glimpse of Thunder
River. Check with the Kaibab Forest Visitors Center in Jacob
Lake for maps and road updates. The forest service maintains
everything north of the rim, which is monitored by the national
park service.

HISTORIC SIGHTS

Grand Canyon Lodge. Originally built in 1928 by the Union
Pacific Railroad, the two-story, Spanish-style lodge burned

down in the early morning hours of September 1, 1932. Rebuilt in 1937 on the original structure's footprint, the new lodge followed the same floor plans with a few changes. The second-story dormitory and the observation station were omitted from the new construction, the new rooflines more steeply pitched, and the exterior architecture less stylized and strictly rustic. Today, the massive stone structure is listed on the National Register of Historic Places. Its huge sunroom has hardwood floors, high-beam ceilings, and a marvelous view of the canyon through plate-glass windows. On warm days, visitors sit outside and drink in the surrounding beauty on an outdoor viewing deck, where National Park Service employees deliver free lectures on geology and history (⇨*Educational Offerings*). ⊠*Off Hwy. 67, near Bright Angel Point.*

SCENIC STOPS

★ **Bright Angel Point.** The trail, which leads to one of the most awe-inspiring overlooks on either rim, starts on the grounds of the Grand Canyon Lodge and runs along the crest of a point of rocks that juts into the canyon for several hundred yards. The walk is only ½-mi round-trip, but it's an exciting trek accented by sheer drops on each side of the trail. In a few spots where the route is extremely narrow, metal railings ensure visitors' safety. The temptation to clamber out to precarious perches to have your picture taken could get you killed–every year several people die from falls at the Grand Canyon. ⊠*North Rim Dr., Grand Canyon.*

Cape Royal. A popular sunset destination, **Cape Royal** showcases the canyon's jagged landscape; you'll also get a glimpse of the Colorado River, framed by a natural stone arch called "Angels Window." In autumn, the aspens turn a beautiful gold, adding even more color to an already magnificent scene of the forested surroundings. At Angels Window Overlook, mi north of here, **Cliff Springs Trail** starts its 1-mi route (round-trip) through a forested ravine. The trail terminates at Cliff Springs, where the forest opens to another impressive view of the canyon walls. ⊠*Cape Royal Rd., 23 mi southeast of Grand Canyon Lodge.*

Point Imperial. At 8,803 feet, Point Imperial has the highest vista point at either rim; it offers magnificent views of both the eastern part of the canyon and the distant country: the Vermilion Cliffs to the north, the 10,000-foot Navajo Mountain to the northeast in Utah, the Painted Desert to

CLOSE UP

Brighty of the Grand Canyon

Cast in bronze, the life-sized statue of a burro sits in the Grand Canyon Lodge sunroom, gazing out at the Grand Canyon through a wall of windows. The statue is modeled after a real-life burro named Brighty, who played a role in Grand Canyon history and roamed the canyon from around 1892 until 1922. Famous children's author Marguerite Henry chronicled this wild burro's life in the book Brighty of the Grand Canyon in 1953. The bronze statue serves as a reminder of this colorful character. While you're here you might notice that the statue's nose is shiny where countless visitors have rubbed it for good luck.

the east, and the confluence of the Little Colorado and Colorado rivers to the southeast. Other prominent points of interest include views of Mt. Hayden, Saddle Mountain, and Marble Canyon. ⊠ *2.7 mi left off Cape Royal Scenic Rd. on Point Imperial Rd., 11 mi northeast of the Grand Canyon Lodge.*

★ **Fodor's Choice Point Sublime.** Talk about solitude. Here you can camp within feet of the canyon's edge. Sunrises and sunsets are spectacular. The western viewpoint sits on the end of a narrow ledge of land stretching 10 mi into the canyon with panoramic views of both the North and South rims, as well as the large rock reef known as Powell Plateau. The winding road, through gorgeous high country, is only 17 mi, but it will take you at least two hours, one-way. The road is intended only for vehicles with high-road clearance (pickups and four-wheel-drive vehicles). It is also necessary to be properly equipped for wilderness road travel; make sure you have a spare tire, a jack, sleeping gear, food, and water. Check with a park ranger or at the information desk at Grand Canyon Lodge before taking this journey. You may camp here only with a permit from the Backcountry Office. ⊠ *North Rim Dr., Grand Canyon; about 20 mi west of North Rim Visitor Center.*

Roosevelt Point. Named after President Roosevelt, who gave the Grand Canyon its national-park status in 1919, this is the best place to see the confluence of the Little Colorado River and the Grand Canyon. The cliffs above the Colorado River south of the junction are the known as the Palisades of the Desert. A short woodland loop trail leads to this eastern viewpoint. ⊠*Cape Royal Rd., 18 mi southeast of the Grand Canyon Lodge.*

Vista Encantada. This viewpoint on the Walhalla Plateau offers views of the upper drainage of Nankoweap Creek, a rock pinnacle known as Brady Peak, and the Painted Desert to the east. This is an enchanting place for a picnic lunch; you'll find several picnic tables near the rim. ⊠*Cape Royal Rd., 16 mi southeast of the Grand Canyon Lodge.*

Walhalla Overlook. One of the lowest elevations on the North Rim, this viewpoint features views of the Unkar Delta, a fertile region used by Ancestral Puebloans as farmland. These ancient people also gathered food and hunted game on the North Rim. A flat path at this overlook leads to the remains of the Walhalla Glades Pueblo, which was inhabited from 1050 to 1150. ⊠*Cape Royal Rd., 22½ mi southeast of the Grand Canyon Lodge.*

EN ROUTE. As you journey to the North Rim from Lees Ferry, the immense blue-green bulk of the Kaibab Plateau stretches out before you. About 18 mi past Navajo Bridge, a sign directs you to the **San Bartolome Historic Site,** an overlook with plaques that tell the story of the Domínguez-Escalante expedition of 1776. At **House Rock Valley,** a large road sign announces the House Rock Buffalo Ranch, operated by the Arizona Game and Fish Department. A 23-mi dirt road leads to the home of one of the largest herds of American bison in the Southwest. You may drive out to the ranch, but be aware that you may not see any buffalo—the expanse of their range is so great that they frequently cannot be spotted from a car. As it nears its junction with Highway 67, U.S. 89A starts climbing to the top of the **Kaibab Plateau,** which is heavily forested, filled with animals and birds, and more than 9,000 feet at its highest point. The rapid change from barren desert to lush forest is dramatic.

DAY HIKES

On the South Rim, all but the paved Rim Trail require strenuous hikes down into the canyon. However, hiking on the North Rim focuses on easy to moderate rim and forest hikes ranging in length from the 0.2-mi woodland loop at Roosevelt Point to the winding 10-mi forested Ken

Stormy Weather

Summer thunderstorms roll across the Colorado Plateau from July through September, bringing much needed precipitation to the Grand Canyon. These fierce displays of nature also bring the risk of lightening, which is more prominent on the higher North Rim. There is an average of 26,073 lighting strikes in Grand Canyon National Park each year. Hair standing on end is a warning; it signals that an electrical charge is building close to you. The safest place to be during a thunderstorm is in a build-ing or in a vehicle with the windows closed. Practice basic safety precautions to reduce the risks of storm-related dangers.

■ Plan ahead and check the weather forecasts to minimize your risk of being struck by lightening.

■ In case of a thunderstorm, move away from the canyon rim and take shelter.

■ When storms are near, do not touch metal guardrails and move away from rocky outcrops, bodies of water, and lone trees.

Patrick Trail leading to Point Imperial. For a day hike into the canyon, travel 5 mi down the North Kaibab Trail to Roaring Springs.

Remember that the canyon has significant elevation changes and, in summer, extreme temperature ranges, which can pose problems for people who aren't in good shape or who have heart or respiratory problems. **Carry plenty of water and energy foods.** The majority of each year's 400 search-and-rescue incidents result from hikers underestimating the size of the canyon, hiking beyond their abilities, or not packing sufficient food and water.

Although permits are not required for day hikes, you must have a backcountry permit for longer trips (⇨ *see Permits under Things to Consider in Grand Canyon Essentials at the end of this book*). Some of the more popular trails are listed in this chapter; more detailed information and maps can be obtained from the North Rim Backcountry Office. Also, rangers can help design a trip to suit your abilities.

SPOTLIGHT HIKE: NORTH KAIBAB TRAIL

At 8,250 feet, the trailhead to North Kaibab Trail is about 2 mi north of the Grand Canyon Lodge. The long, steep

GREAT ITINERARIES

NORTH RIM IN 1 DAY

Get oriented by starting your day with a visit to the **North Rim Visitor Center** near Grand Canyon Lodge and check out the day's scheduled ranger programs. Take the short walk to **Bright Angel Point** for your first views of the Grand Canyon from the North Rim. Pack a picnic lunch and head along Point Imperial Road to **Point Imperial,** the highest point on either rim at 8,803 feet. Next, take a drive down Cape Royal Road and head south to **Vista Encantada,** which offers wide views of the Painted Desert and Brady Peak. Just south is **Roosevelt Point,** which is accessed by a short woodland loop trail. The next stop is at **Walhalla Overlook,** where you can take a walking tour of the prehistoric Indian Ruins at Walhalla Glades. The final stop is at **Cape Royal,** the only developed North Rim overlook with a view of the Colorado River. You'll also have striking views of Horseshoe Mesa, Wotans Throne, Vishnu Temple, and Freya Castle. The short paved **Cape Royal Trail** has a spur walking out to Angel's Window, a favorite spot to watch the sunset.

NORTH RIM IN 3 DAYS

On Day 1, follow the one-day itinerary and end it with a scheduled ranger-led evening program at **Grand Canyon Lodge.** Spend Day 2 exploring the remote **Point Sublime,** the westernmost of the North Rim viewpoints. On Day 3, take a day hike on one of the rim trails or head down into the canyon to Roaring Springs on the **North Kaibab Trail.** It takes twice as long to hike back up, so plan accordingly. Pick up trail maps at the **North Rim Visitor Center,** and bring plenty of water.

path follows the Bright Angel Fault and drops 5,850 feet over a distance of 14½ mi to the Colorado River. The National Park Service suggests that day hikers not go farther than Roaring Springs (5,020 feet) before turning to hike back up out of the canyon; allow eight hours roundtrip. Because the North Rim is 1,000 feet higher than the South Rim, hikers looking to take a rim-to-rim trip often descend the North Kaibab Trail and return up one of the shorter southern trails; allow three to four nights roundtrip. ⊠ *Trailhead is approx. 2 mi north of Grand Canyon Lodge on North Rim Rd.* ☞ *Moderate to difficult.*

0.7 MI: COCONINO OVERLOOK

The first leg of this trail is popular with day hikers. It quickly descends from the Kaibab formation at the trail-head to the top of the Coconino Sandstone. From the over-look you can see Roaring Springs Canyon and the distant South Rim.

2 MI: SUPAI TUNNEL

Steep switchbacks lead to this tunnel, which was blasted through the Supai Group in the 1930s by the Civilian Conservation Corps when this section of trail was rerouted. This resting point has seasonal water and restrooms.

5 MI: ROARING SPRINGS

The next 3 mi follow the Bright Angel Fault through Redwall Limestone. Along the way you'll cross a bridge built in 1966 when a flood wiped out a section of the trail. Roaring Springs provides water for both rims. This is as far as you should travel on a day hike.

6.8 MI: COTTONWOOD CAMP

The next 1½ mi travel through the Tapeats Narrows before coming to this seasonal campground at 4,080 feet. Named for the cottonwood trees that grow here, this campground has a ranger station, drinking water in summer, restrooms, and picnic tables.

8.1 MI: RIBBON FALLS

Desert vegetation dominates the landscape as the trail continues further into the canyon. A spur off the main trail leads 0.3 mi to the oasis at Ribbon Falls. Footing can be hazardous when crossing the stream. Camping is not permitted at this day site.

13.8 MI: PHANTOM RANCH

The last 5.7 mi winds down 1,500 feet to historic Phantom Ranch, a popular destination for rim-to-river hikers on both sides of the canyon. Phantom Ranch is open year-round and has drinking water, restrooms, and an emergency phone. There is also a pay phone available. Reservations for food and lodging at Phantom Ranch must be made in advance.

OTHER HIKES

Cape Final Trail. This easy 2-mi hike follows an old jeep trail through a ponderosa-pine forest to the canyon overlook at Cape Final. The lightly visited overlook features panoramic

NORTH KAIBAB TRAIL TIPS

■ The North Kaibab Trail is the only maintained trail into the canyon from the North Rim.

■ Most day hikers should go only as far as Coconino Overlook (1.5-mi round-trip) or the Supai Tunnel (2-mi round-trip). Roaring Springs (10-mi round-trip) is the maximum distance recommended for a day hike.

■ Rangers suggest scheduling a minimum of three nights for a round-trip hike from the North Rim to the South Rim.

■ For a fee, a shuttle takes hikers to the North Kaibab trailhead twice daily. Reservations are required.

■ Water is available at Supai Tunnel and Cottonwood Camp May through September. Phantom Ranch has drinking water year-round.

■ Emergency phones are located at Cottonwood Camp and Phantom Ranch.

views of the northern canyon, the Palisades of the Desert, and the impressive spectacle of Juno Temple. ✉ *For trailhead, park at the dirt parking lot located 5 mi south of Roosevelt Point on Cape Royal Rd.* ☞ *Easy.*

☾ ★ **Cape Royal Trail.** Informative signs on natural history add to this popular 0.6-mi, one-way paved path to Cape Royal; allow 30 minutes round-trip. Located at an elevation of 7,685 feet on the southern edge of the Walhalla Plateau, this popular viewpoint offers expansive views of Wotans Throne, Vishnu Temple, Freya Castle, Horseshoe Mesa, and the Colorado River. The trail also offers several nice views of Angels Window. ✉ *Trailhead at the southeast side of Cape Royal parking area* ☞ *Easy.*

Clear Creek Trail. Make this 9-mi hike only if you are prepared for a multiday trip. This trail departs from Phantom Ranch at the bottom of the canyon, crosses the Colorado River to the North Rim side, and leads across the Tonto Platform to Clear Creek, where drinking water is usually available, but should be treated. ✉ *Trailhead is ¼ mi north of Phantom Ranch along the North Kaibab Trail (marked by a wooden sign)* ☞ *Moderate.*

☾ **Cliff Springs Trail.** An easy 1-mi (round-trip), 1-hour walk near Cape Royal, Cliff Springs Trail leads through a forested ravine to an excellent view of the canyon. The trailhead begins across from Angels Window Overlook.

Narrow and precarious in spots, it passes ancient dwellings, winds beneath a limestone overhang, and ends at Cliff Springs. ⊠ *Trailhead is across from a small pullout 0.3 mi down the road from Cape Royal* ☞ *Easy.*

Ken Patrick Trail. This primitive trail begins at a trailhead on the east side of the North Kaibab trailhead parking lot. It travels 10-mi, one-way (allow 6 hours) from the trailhead at 8,250 feet to Point Imperial at 8,803 feet. It crosses drainages and occasionally detours around fallen trees. The end of the road brings the highest views from either rim at Point Imperial. Note that there is no water along this trail. ⊠ *Trailhead at Point Imperial parking area* ☞ *Moderate.*

Nankoweap Trail. Accessed by a 3½-mi hike on Forest Service Trail 57 or 2 mi from Point Imperial on Point Imperial Trail, the National Park trailhead actually begins at Saddle Mountain Point at an elevation on 7,560 feet. Following an old Paiute route, Nankoweap Trail edges along a perilous precipice, scrambles down a rocky ridge, and passes prehistoric Indian ruins and gardens on the Nankoweap Creek delta before continuing down to the river's edge. ⊠ *Trailhead off Forest Service Rd. 610, 4.6 mi north of the North Rim entrance* ☞ *Difficult.*

NEWS FLASH. Flash floods can occur any time of the year, especially from June through September when thunderstorms develop rapidly. Check forecasts before heading into the canyon, never camp in dry washes, and use caution when hiking in narrow canyons and drainage systems.

North Bass Trail. Accessible by four-wheel drive vehicles off Swamp Point Road, this wilderness trail descends from the trailhead at 7,500 feet in a series of steep switchbacks to Muav Saddle, where it branches left to follow White Creek. The route descends through the Tapeats Narrows to Shinumo Creek, where the trail continues down to the Colorado River. This 14-mi hike is considered to be one of the most strenuous trails in the canyon and should only be attempted by experienced hikers. Just getting to the trailhead is a chore, a 2-hour drive down Swamp Point Rd. ⊠ *Trailhead at Swamp Point, which is reachable from DeMotte Park via Forest Service Rds. 22, 270, 223, 268, 268B, and Swamp Point Rd., in the Kaibab National Forest* ☞ *Very Difficult.*

Point Imperial Trail. This easy 2-mi, one-way trail travels from Point Imperial, the highest point on the North Rim at 8,803 feet, to the northern park boundary at Saddle Mountain, where you can connect with the Nankoweap Trail. The level trail passes through some fire-damaged areas burned by the 2000 Outlet Fire. A restroom and picnic tables are located at the trailhead. ⊠ *Trailhead is at Point Imperial parking area* ☞ *Easy.*

Roosevelt Point Trail. Located at Roosevelt Point on Cape Royal Road, this easy 0.2-mi, round-trip trail loops through the forest to the scenic viewpoint. Allow 20 minutes for this short, secluded hike. ⊠ *Trailhead is at Roosevelt Point, Cape Royal Rd.* ☞ *Easy.*

Thunder River Trail. This long 15-mi, one-way trail departs from Indian Hollow (off Forest Service Road 232), winds down steep switchbacks, and travels past crashing waterfalls before dropping down into Surprise Valley. This wilderness trail can be extremely hot and dry during the summer months, reaching temperatures as high as 120°F. There are two campgrounds on the trail, Lower Tapeats Campground near the river, and Upper Tapeats Campground, which has restrooms. For a variation on the hike, take the Deer Creek Trail from Surprise Valley. This side trail enters a deep, narrow canyon and follows a ledge along the creek before descending down a talus slope to the base of Deer Creek Falls and the Colorado River. ⊠ *Trailhead at Indian Hollow (off Forest Service Rd. 232), off U.S. 89A a few miles east of Fredonia, AZ* ☞ *Difficult.*

ROARING WATERS. Measuring only a ½ mi in length, Thunder River is the shortest river in the world. It erupts from its spring-fed source in Thunder Cave, spilling 1,200 feet down the canyon in a dramatic rush of water before coming to a sudden end at its confluence with Tapeats Creek.

Transept Trail. This 3-mi (round-trip), 1½-hour trail begins at 8,255 feet near the Grand Canyon Lodge's east patio. Well-maintained and marked, it has little elevation change, sticking near the rim before reaching a dramatic view of a large stream through Bright Angel Canyon. The route leads to a side canyon called Transept Canyon, which geologist Clarence Dutton named in 1882, declaring it "far grander than Yosemite." Check the posted schedule to find a ranger talk along this trail; it's also a great place to view fall foliage. ⊠ *Trailhead at Grand Canyon Lodge east patio* ☞ *Easy.*

Uncle Jim Trail. This 5-mi, 3-hour loop trail starts at the North Kaibab Trail parking lot at 8,300 feet and winds south through the forest, past Roaring Springs Canyon and Bright Angel Canyon. The highlight of this rim hike is Uncle Jim Point, which, at 8,244 feet, overlooks the upper sections of the North Kaibab Trail. ⊠ *Trailhead at North Kaibab Trail parking lot, which is approx. 2 mi north of Grand Canyon Lodge on North Rim Rd.* ☞ *Moderate.*

★ **Widforss Trail.** Round-trip, Widforss Trail is 9 8/10 mi, with an elevation change of 200 feet. The trailhead, at 8,100 feet, is across from the North Kaibab Trail parking lot. Allow six hours for the hike, which passes through shady forests of pine, spruce, fir, and aspen on its way to Widforss Point, at 7,900 feet. Here you'll have good views of five temples: Zoroaster, Brahma, and Deva to the southeast and Buddha and Manu to the southwest. You are likely to see wildflowers in summer, and this is a good trail for viewing fall foliage. It's named in honor of artist Gunnar M. Widforss, renowned for his paintings of national-park landscapes. ⊠ *Trailhead at Widforss Trail parking area; take the dirt road ¼ mi south of Cape Royal Road for 1 mi* ☞ *Moderate.*

SUMMER SPORTS & ACTIVITIES

BICYCLING

Mountain bikers can test the many dirt access roads found in this remote area, including the 17-mi trek to Point Sublime. It's rare to spot other people on these primitive roads. Schwinn bicycles can be rented by the hour at the North Rim Outfitters Station (⊠ *Grand Canyon Lodge, North Rim 86052* ☎ *877/386–4383 ext. 758* ⊕ *www.grandcanyonforever.com*). Bicycles and leashed pets are allowed on the 1.2-mi (one-way) **Bridle Trail,** which follows the road from Grand Canyon Lodge to the North Kaibab Trailhead. Bikes are prohibited on all other national-park trails.

★ For another off-road option, ride the **Rainbow Rim Trail,** an 18-mi, one-way trail that begins at Parissawampitts Point at the end of Forest Road 214 and ends at Timp Point on Forest Road 271. This premier trail also includes stops

3

HIKING TRAILS AT A GLANCE

	Grade	Miles (one-way)	Beginning Elevation (feet)	Ending Elevation (feet)	Mules	Campground	Open Info	Water	Shuttle Access	Range Station	Toilet/ Restroom	Emergency Telephone	Level	Conditions
Clear Creek Trail	Incline	9	2600	3600	N	Y	Y/R	Y	N	N	N	N	Mod.	Unmaintained
Ken Patrick Trail	Level/ Incline	10	8250	8803	N	N	Y/R	Y	Y	N	Y	Y	Easy	Maintained
Nankoweap Trail	Steep	11	7560	2760	N	N	mid-May–mid-Oct.	N	N	N	N	N	Diff.	Unmaintained
North Bass Trail	Steep	14	7500	2200	N	N	mid-May–mid-Oct.	N	N	N	N	N	Diff.	Unmaintained
North Kaibab Trail	Steep	14.2	8250	2400	Y	Y	mid-May–mid-Oct.	Y	Y	Y	Y	Y	Mod./Diff.	Maintained
Thunder River Trail	Very Steep	15	6400	2000	N	Y	mid-May–mid-Oct.	N	N	N	Y	N	Diff.	Unmaintained
Transept Trail	Level	1.5	8255	8200	N	N	mid-May–mid-Oct.	N	N	N	Y	Y	Easy	Maintained
Uncle Jim Trail	Level	2.5	8300	8244	Y	N	mid-May–mid-Oct.	N	N	N	N	N	Easy	Maintained
Widforss Trail	Level/ Incline	5	8100	7900	N	N	mid-May–mid-Oct.	N	N	N	N	N	Easy	Maintained

* Water is seasonal **at trailhead only Y/R = year-round M = Maintained U = Unmaintained

at three other fantastic viewpoints—Fence, Locust, and North Timp—winding through a ponderosa-pine forest and up and down side canyons, aspen groves, and pristine meadows. The trail's elevation of 7,550 feet doesn't vary more than 200 feet along the way. The Rainbow Rim Trail is in the Kaibab National Forest and closed to motorized vehicles.

HORSEBACK RIDING

Private livestock is limited to the corridor trail (North Kaibab Trail) in the inner canyon and on select rim trails including Uncle Jim Trail. Bright Angel and Cottonwood Campgrounds accommodate private equines as does the North Rim Horse Camp, located ¼ mi from the North Kaibab Trailhead. Grazing is not permitted; handlers are required to pack their own feed. A backcountry permit is required for any overnight use of private stock.

MULE RIDES

OUTFITTER

☺ **Canyon Trail Rides.** This company leads mule rides on the easier trails of the North Rim. A one-hour ride (minimum age 7) runs $30. Half-day trips on the rim or into the canyon (minimum age 10) cost $65; full-day trips (minimum age 12) go for $125. Weight limits vary from 200 to 220 pounds. Available daily from May 15 to October 15, these excursions are popular, so make reservations in advance. ☏ *435/679–8665* ⊕ *www.canyonrides.com.*

RAFTING

★ **Fodor's Choice** Those who have taken a white-water-raft trip down the Colorado River often say it is one of their most memorable life experiences. Most trips begin at Lees Ferry, a few miles below the Glen Canyon Dam near Page. There are tranquil half- and full-day float trips from the Glen Canyon Dam to Lees Ferry, as well as raft trips that run from 7 to 18 days. Many of these voyages end at Phantom Ranch at the bottom of the Grand Canyon at river mile 87. You'll encounter some good white water along the way, including Lava Falls, listed in the *Guinness Book of World Records* as "the fastest navigable white water stretch in North America."

Rafting Basics

So you're ready to tackle the churning white water of the Colorado River as it rumbles and hisses its way through the Grand Canyon? Well, you're in good company: The crafty, one-armed Civil War veteran John Wesley Powell first charted these dangerous rapids during the summer of 1869. It wasn't until 1938, though, that the first commercial river trip made its way down this fearsome corridor. Running the river has come a long way since then—and since Norman Neville made the first trip by kayak, in 1941, in a craft he built out of scrap lumber salvaged from an outhouse and a run-down barn.

White-water rafting still offers all the excitement of those early days—without the danger and discomfort. Professional river runners lead journeys ranging from relaxing half-day float trips to adventurous 18-day oar excursions. Lifejackets, beverages, tents, sheets, tarps, sleeping bags, wet bags, first-aid, and food are provided—but you'll still need to plan ahead by packing clothing, hats, sunscreen, toiletries, and other sundries. Keep in mind that seats fill up fast due to the restricted number of visitors allowed on the river each season by the National Park Service. But once you've secured your seat, all that's left to do is pack your bags and get geared up for an experience of a lifetime. Lots of people book trips for summer's peak period: June through August. If you're flexible, take advantage of the Arizona weather; May to early June and September are ideal rafting times in the Grand Canyon.

Sixteen companies (at the time of this writing) offer motorized and oar-powered excursions, but reservations for raft trips (excluding smooth-water, one-day cruises) often need to be made more than six months in advance. Prices for river-raft trips vary greatly, depending on type and length. Half-day trips on smooth water run as low as $118 per adult/$65 for children. Trips that negotiate the entire length of the canyon and take as long as 12 days can cost more than $3,000.

OUTFITTERS & EXPEDITIONS

Reputable outfitters include **Arizona River Runners** (☎602/867–4866 or 800/477–7238 ⊕*www.raftarizona.com*), **Canyoneers, Inc.** (☎928/526–0924, 800/525–0924 *outside Arizona* ⊕*www.canyoneers.com*), **Diamond River Adventures, Inc.** (☎928/645–8866 or 800/343–3121 ⊕*www.*

diamondriver.com), **Grand Canyon Expeditions Company** (☎435/644–2691 or 800/544–2691 ⊕*www.gcex.com*), **Tour West, Inc.** (☎801/225–0755 or 800/453–9107 ⊕*www.twriver.com*), and **Wilderness River Adventures** (☎928/645–3279 or 800/992–8022 ⊕*www.riveradventures.com*).

WINTER SPORTS & ACTIVITIES

Due to heavy snows and extreme winter weather, the North Rim closes all of its services from mid-October through mid-May. However, Highway 67 stays open to the North Rim until snows force the closure of the road at Jacob Lake. After the road closes, the rim can be accessed by hiking, snowshoeing, and cross-country skiing. A backcountry permit is required for winter overnight use of the North Rim from the park's northern boundary to Bright Angel Point on the canyon rim.

EXPLORING THE BACKCOUNTRY

Of the 4.5 million people traveling to Grand Canyon National Park each year, only a small fraction spend more than a day exploring the rim, and even fewer actually explore its secrets on an overnight trip into its depths. The park encompasses more than 1.2 million acres, but only a small portion of this rugged countryside can be accessed by hikers. Each year more than 30,000 overnight-permit requests flood the Backcountry Information Center but, only 13,000 permits are issued. Due to the fragile desert environment and careful monitoring by the park service, the demand usually exceeds permit availability. The Colorado River separates the South Rim and the North Rim, with the only river crossing at Phantom Ranch. The best seasons to hike the canyon are in the spring and fall, which are also the most difficult time to obtain a permit. Be sure to allow twice as much time to ascend the canyon as it did to hike down. Because the longer hiking distances from the North Rim to the Colorado River, rangers suggest a minimum of three nights for a round-trip hike from the North Rim to the Colorado River.

Backcountry Information Center. Backcountry permits are required for overnight horseback-riding trips and for overnight use of the North Rim Horse Camp. To increase your chances for obtaining a permit, make your request as early

Freebies at the Canyon

While you're here, be sure to take advantage of the many freebies offered at Grand Canyon National Park. Ranger-led programs are always free and offered mid-May through mid-October. There are usually at least four ranger programs held daily. These programs might include activities such as stargazing and guided hikes and topics such as geology and the cultural history of prehistoric peoples. Some of the more in-depth programs may include a fossil walk or a condor talk. Check with the visitor center for seasonal programs including wildflower walks and fire ecology.

3

as possible. Reservations are taken up to four months in advance. Contact Grand Canyon National Park's Backcountry Information Center for a copy of the *Backcountry Trip Planner*. ⌂*Box 129, Grand Canyon 86023* ☎*928/638 7875* 📠*928/638-2125* ⊕*www.nps.gov/grca* 💲*$5 per stock animal per night* ▤*AE, D, MC, V* ♿*Reservations essential.*

EDUCATIONAL PROGRAMS

Learn about prehistoric cultures, take an interpretive guided hike, learn about condor conservation, and uncover the layered geologic history of the canyon with scheduled ranger programs. Outdoor programs can be cancelled due to bad weather; always check ahead.

RANGER PROGRAMS

Condor Talk. Learn about the reintroduction of the endangered California condor and ongoing conservation efforts. Meet a park ranger at the fireplace on the back porch of the Grand Canyon Lodge; allow 30 minutes. ☎*928/638–7888* ⊕*www.nps.gov/grca* 💲*Free.*

☙ **Discovery Pack Junior Ranger Program.** Children ages 9 to 14 can take part in these hands-on educational programs and earn a Junior Ranger certificate and badge. ☎*928/638–7888* ⊕*www.nps.gov/grca/forkids/index.htm* 💲*Free.*

Interpretive Ranger Programs. Daily guided hikes and talks may focus on any aspect of the canyon—from geology and flora and fauna to history and the canyon's early inhabitants. For schedules, go to the Grand Canyon Lodge or pick up a free copy of *The Guide* to the North Rim. ☎ *928/638–7888* ⊕ *www.nps.gov/grca*.

Into the Past. Take an in-depth look at the ancient inhabitants of the North Rim. This ranger-led program includes a guided tour of the excavated ruins at Walhalla Glades. Meet a park ranger at the Walhalla Overlook, 22½ mi from Grand Canyon Lodge on Cape Royal Road; allow 45 minutes. ☎ *928/638–7888* ⊕ *www.nps.gov/grca* ▤ *Free*.

What's Rockin'?—Grand Canyon Geology. Get the dirt on the geological makeup of the Grand Canyon. After the talk, take a guided hike to Bright Angel Point for a first-hand look of the canyon's layered history. Meet a park ranger at the fireplace on the back porch of the Grand Canyon Lodge; allow 60 minutes. ☎ *928/638–7888* ⊕ *www.nps. gov/grca* ▤ *Free*.

PETS AT THE NORTH RIM. Pets are allowed in Grand Canyon National Park; however, they must be on a leash at all times. With the exception of service animals, pets are not allowed below the rim or on any park trails other than the Bridle Trail, which connects Grand Canyon Lodge with the North Kaibab Trail. There is no kennel on the North Rim and pets are not permitted in the Grand Canyon Lodge.

ARTS & ENTERTAINMENT

Evening Program. End your day with a one-hour evening presentation on the canyon's natural or cultural history. Presentations are held daily at 8 PM at the Grand Canyon Lodge auditorium. Nightly topics are posted at the lodge, campground, and visitor center. ☎ *928/638–7610* ⊕ *www. nps.gov/grca*.

Roughrider Saloon. Pull up a stool and have a drink at this rustic lounge in the Grand Canyon Lodge complex. A large glass window encourages people-watching and historic photos line the walls. The bar is open daily from 11:30 AM to 11 PM. ✉ *Grand Canyon Lodge* ☎ *928/638–2611*.

FESTIVALS & EVENTS

Held in mid-July **Western Arts Day** celebrates the Western culture of northern Arizona and southern Utah. The day-long event includes cowboy poetry readings, musical performances, and craft demonstrations. Check at the visitor center for a complete listing of activities.

The annual **Native American Heritage Days,** held the first weekend in August, features Native American groups indigenous to the Grand Canyon and the Colorado Plateau. Activities include craft demonstrations, educational lectures, guided hikes, Indian arts and crafts, and Native American song and dance. This festival originally began as "Paiute Days" in 1993 to honor the last native group to occupy the North Rim area on a seasonal basis. In 1997, the event was expanded to include all native groups with cultural ties to the Grand Canyon.

Exploring the West Rim

4

WORD OF MOUTH

"We have hiked many times to Havasupai. You won't get lost on the trail. The lodge is 2 miles from the waterfalls. We have been to the 3 waterfalls many times. June is the best time to go. Definitely swimming is best at Navajo Falls."

—marymarathons

By Carrie
Miner

KNOWN AS "THE PEOPLE" OF THE GRAND CANYON,
the Pai Indians—the Havasupai and Hualapai—have lived
along the Colorado River and the vast Colorado Plateau
for more than 1,000 years. Both the Havasupai and the
Hualapai seasonally moved between the plateau and the
canyon, alternately hunting game and planting crops.
Today, both tribes rely on tourism as an economic base.

With the establishment of Grand Canyon National Park in
1919, the Havasupai people were confined to their summer village of Supai and the surrounding 518 acres in the
5-mi-wide, 12-mi-long Havasu Canyon. In 1975, the reservation was substantially enlarged, but is still completely
surrounded by national-park lands on all but its southern
border. Each year, about 25,000 tourists fly, hike, or ride
into Havasu Canyon to visit the Havasupai ("people of
the blue green water"). Despite their economic reliance
on tourism, the Havasupai take their guardianship of the
Grand Canyon seriously, and severely limit visitation in
order to protect the fragile canyon habitats. Dubbed the
"Shangri-la of the Grand Canyon," the remote, inacces-
sible Indian reservation includes some of the world's most
beautiful and famous waterfalls, together with streams and
pools tinted a mystical blue-green by dissolved travertine.

The plateau-dwelling Hualapai ("people of the tall pines")
acquired a larger chunk of traditional Pai lands with the
creation of their reservation in 1883. Although the tribe
only has about 2,400 members, the Hualapai Reservation
encompasses 108 mi of the Colorado River and a million
acres of the Grand Canyon and its surrounding southern
plateaus. Hualapai tribal lands include diverse habitats
ranging from rolling grasslands to rugged canyons, and
travel from elevations of 1,500 feet at the Colorado River
to more than 7,300 feet at Aubrey Cliffs. In recent years,
the Hualapai have been attempting to foster tourism on the
West Rim—most notably with the spectacular Skywalk, a
glass walkway suspended over the edge of the canyon rim.
Not hampered by the regulations in place at Grand Canyon National Park, Destination Grand Canyon West offers
helicopter flights down into the canyon, horseback rides to
rim viewpoints, and boat trips up the Colorado River.

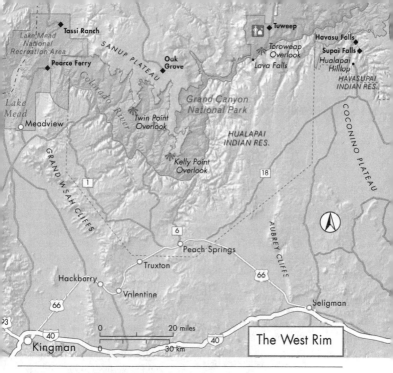

EXPLORING THE WEST RIM

GRAND CANYON WEST

70 mi north of Kingman via Stockton Hill Rd., Pierce Ferry Rd., and Diamond Bar Rd.

The Hualapai Reservation encompasses a million acres along 108 mi of the Colorado River in the Grand Canyon. Peach Springs, located on historic Route 66, is the tribal capital and the location of the Hualapai Lodge (the pickup point for white-water-raft tours). The increasingly popular West Rim is more than 120 mi away on freeway roads. However, visitors taking tour options from the Hualapai Lodge take a motor-coach tour on the shorter 49-mi tribal route along Buck and Doe Road.

At the West Rim, which is a five-hour drive from the South Rim of Grand Canyon National Park, the Hualapai Tribe offers a wide variety of tour packages. Visitors aren't allowed to travel in their own vehicles once they reach the West Rim but must purchase a tour package. The basic

GREAT ITINERARIES

THE WEST RIM IN 1 DAY

Hop on the Grand Canyon West Express shuttle and head to **Eagle Point** for your first views of Grand Canyon West. Discover an array of Native lifestyle at the different dwellings in Indian Village, watch impromptu Native American dance programs at Eagle Plaza or the nearby amphitheater, and get a natural high with stunning views from the popular **Skywalk**. The next stop on the shuttle route is at **Guano Point** where you can take a short hike with canyon overlooks, peruse Native American arts and crafts at an outdoor marketplace, and take a lunch break at the Hualapai Buffet. Next, hop back on the shuttle and head to **Hualapai Ranch** for a horseback ride to Quartermaster Point or return to the visitors center to schedule an off-road Hummer tour or an inner canyon excursion, which includes a helicopter trip into the canyon and a boat tour up the Colorado River.

THE WEST RIM IN 3 DAYS

After following Day 1's itinerary, drive to Peach Springs for the night. On the second morning, head to Hualapai Hilltop and hike the **Havasu Trail** down to the Havasupai village of Supai. Spend the afternoon setting up camp and exploring the blue-green waterfalls in **Havasu Canyon**. Spend the morning on Day 3 playing in the travertine pools and take it easy on the return trip with a horseback ride or a helicopter lift out of the canyon. You'll need a Havasupai tribal permit to hike here.

Alternately, make your trip to **Havasu Canyon** a day trip by taking a helicopter flight in and out of the canyon. You'll have a few hours to explore one or two of the three famous waterfalls before catching a return flight. The next day, raft the Class V and VI rapids on the Colorado River and take a short side hike to Travertine Falls with **Hualapai River Runners**.

Hualapai Legacy Package ($29.95 per person plus $20 parking fee per vehicle) includes shuttle transportation to Eagle Point, Hualapai Ranch, and Guano Point. Add-ons include horseback or wagon rides to the rim, a helicopter trip into the canyon, a rafting trip on the Colorado River, an off-road Hummer adventure, or a walk oon the Skywalk. Meals and overnight trips can also be added. The Hualapai Tribe requires visitors to obtain permits to travel on tribal lands, although no permit is required to drive to the West Rim if you take a tour while there.

Exploring Indian Country

When visiting Indian reservations, respect tribal laws and customs. Remember you are a guest in a sovereign nation. Do not wander into residential areas or take photographs or residents without first asking permission. In general, the Hualapai and Havasupai are quiet, private people. Offer respect and do not pursue conversations or personal interactions unless invited to do so.

■ Sobering Consequences: Possessing or consuming alcoholic beverages is illegal on Havasupai and Hualapai tribal lands.

■ Stay on Track: Hiking or camping outside established areas is prohibited.

■ Look, but Don't Touch: Removing, disturbing, or destroying archaeological objects is illegal under state, federal, and tribal laws.

Diamond Creek Road, directly north of the Hualapai Lodge in Peach Springs, is the only road into the Grand Canyon (other than Lees Ferry 226 river miles upriver) accessible by private vehicle. The road ends at the Colorado River above Diamond Creek Rapid at river mile 226, which is 138 mi downstream from Phantom Ranch (as the crow flies the distance is about half of that). Diamond Creek Road can be braved by high-clearance passenger vehicles, but your best bet is four-wheel-drive, especially in summer when storms are common.

This vast reservation encompasses an array of diverse habitats ranging from rolling hills and pine forests to sheer cliffs and rugged canyons. This is a popular destination for big-game hunters seeking to bag a desert bighorn sheep—one of the four sheep in the Grand Slam of North American Wild Sheep. **Hualapai Wildlife Conservation** (☎928/769–2230 or 888/255–9550) sells big-game hunting permits for desert bighorn sheep, elk, antelope, and mountain lion.

The Hualapai Tribe's efforts to expand its tourism offerings at the West Rim include the **Skywalk,** a cantilever-shaped glass bridge suspended 4,000 feet above the Colorado River and extending 70 feet from the edge of the Grand Canyon—talk about a cliffhanger! Located at Eagle Point, it opened March 20, 2007. The Skywalk is approximately 10-feet wide, and the bridge's deck, made of tempered glass several inches thick, has 5-foot glass railings on each side. Visitors must store all personal effects, including cameras, cell phones, and video cameras, in lockers ($1 fee) before entering the Skywalk. A professional photographer on the walkway will take personal photographs which can be purchased from the gift shop.

At this writing, a 3-level, 6,000-square-foot visitor's center was under construction at the site. Slated to be completed in late 2008, it will include a museum, movie theater, VIP lounge, gift shop, and several restaurants and bars. A short walk takes visitors to the Indian Village, where educational displays uncover the culture of five different Native American tribes (Havasupai, Plains, Hopi, Hualapai, and Navajo). Intertribal, powwow-style dance performances entertain visitors at the nearby amphitheater.

The dusty, 14-mi stretch of unpaved road leading to Grand Canyon West cannot be made by private vehicle. Visitors can schedule Park & Ride services from the **Grand Canyon West Welcome Center** (⊠ *Pierce Ferry Rd., Peach Springs* ☎*702/260–6506*) for a nominal fee; reservations are required.

Destination Grand Canyon West (☎*702/878–9378 or 877/716–9378*) is the tour operator of the Hualapai Nation, and offers all-inclusive packages departing from Las Vegas and Phoenix.

Destination Grand Canyon West ⊠ *Peach Springs, on the West Rim of the Canyon, 86434* ☎*702/878–9378* ⊕*www.destinationgrandcanyon.com* ⊠*$29.95–$219; Skywalk $29.95, added to any package; additional $20 per vehicle for parking* ⊙*Summer, daily 7* AM*–8* PM*; winter, daily 8–4:30.*

EN ROUTE. As you travel north from Kingman, keep an eye out for the strange-looking namesakes of the **Joshua Tree Forest** (*Yucca brevifolia*). This native of the dry Mojave Desert isn't actually a tree, but instead a member of the lily family. Standing as tall as 40 feet, the alien-looking plant can be recognized by its gangly limbs ending in dense clumps of dark green, bayonet-shaped leaves. Mormon immigrants traveling through the area in the mid-19th century named the towering plants after the biblical figure Joshua. From February through March, Joshua trees blossom in clusters of creamy white blossoms. The trees don't branch until after they bloom and, because they rely on perfect conditions to flower, they don't necessarily bloom every year.

HAVASU CANYON

141 mi from Williams (to Hualapai Hilltop), west on I–40 and AZ 66, north on Indian Hwy. 18. Note: last gas is at junction of AZ 66 and Indian Hwy. 18.

Havasu Canyon, south of the middle part of Grand Canyon National Park's South Rim and away from the crowds, is the home of the Havasupai, a tribe that has lived in this isolated area for centuries. Their name means "people of the blue-green waters," and you'll know why when you see the canyon's waterfalls, as high as 200 feet, cascading over red cliffs into travertine pools surrounded by thick foliage and sheltering cottonwood trees.

The striking falls, plunging into deep turquoise pools, seem like something from Hawai'i or Shangri La. The travertine in the water coats the walls and lines the pools with bizarre, drip castle-rock formations. Centuries of accumulated travertine formations in some of the most popular pools were washed out in massive flooding decades ago, destroying some of the otherworldly scenes pictured in older photos, but the place is still magical.

The 600 tribal members now live in Supai, accessible only down the 8-mi-long **Havasu Trail,** which drops 2,000 feet from the canyon rim to the tiny town; other trails branch off from Supai. The quiet and private Havasupai mostly remain apart from the modest flow of tourists, which nevertheless plays a vital role in the tribal economy.

To reach Havasu's waterfalls, you must hike downstream from the village of Supai. The first fall, 1½ mi from Supai, is the 75-foot-high **Navajo Falls,** named after a 19th-century Havasupai chief who was abducted as a child and raised by the Navajo until he eventually discovered his origin and returned to his tribe as an adult. Navajo Falls rushes over red-wall limestone and collects in a beautiful blue-green pool perfect for swimming. Not much farther downstream, the striking **Havasu Falls** dash over a ledge into another pool of refreshing 70°F water. The last of the enchanting waterfalls is **Mooney Falls,** 2 mi down from Navajo Falls. Mooney Falls, named after a prospector who fell to his death here in 1880, plummets 196 feet down a sheer travertine cliff. The hike down to the pool below is a steep descent down slippery rocks with only the assistance of chains suspended along a series of iron stakes.

The Havasupai restrict the number of visitors to the canyon; you must have reservations, and it's necessary to make reservations for some times of the year far in advance (they are taken up to one year in advance). You can hike into Havasu Canyon on the Havasu Trail. From an elevation of 5,200 feet, the trail travels down a moderate grade to Supai village at 3,200 feet. Bring plenty of water and avoid hiking during the middle of the day, when canyon temperatures can reach into the 100s. Havasu Canyon trail is not a casual day hike; you'll have to spend the night. Once in the canyon, you have the choice of camping or staying in the Havasupai Lodge, which also serves meals to hikers who aren't staying in the lodge (⇨ see Lodging & Dining in the Park in Chapter 5). If hiking isn't your thing, you can also ride a helicopter or horse (⇨ see Air Tours and Horseback Riding in Summer Sports & Activities, below). Visitors to Supai and Havasu Canyon are expected to respect the land and its people. The tribe does not allow alcohol, drugs, pets, or weapons.[]

MAIL BY MULE. Arguably, the most remote mail route in the United States follows a steep 8-mi trail to the tiny town of Supai in Havasu Canyon. Havasupai tribal members living deep within the confines of the Grand Canyon rely on this route for the delivery of everything from food to furniture. During a typical week, more than a ton of mail is sent into the canyon by mule, with each animal carrying a cargo of about 130 pounds.

BACKCOUNTRY HIKES

SPOTLIGHT HIKE: HAVASU TRAIL

The Havasu Trail is the main route to the remote Havasupai village of Supai. The trip from Hualapai Hilltop to the pastoral village normally takes three hours; allow an extra hour for the ascent. The trail begins at an elevation of 5,200 feet at Hualapai Hilltop and descends to 3,200 feet at Supai. Horse traffic is often heavy along this part of the trail; horses have the right-of-way on this narrow path. After the initial descent, the trail continues to wind down through the village to the campground and past the canyon's famous waterfalls. ✉ *Trailhead at Hualapai Hilltop, which is 68 mi north of Rte. 66, which branches off of*

I–40 at Kingman on the west or Seligman on the east, via Indian Rd. 18 ☞ *Moderate.*

6½ MI: HAVASU CREEK

The first portion of the trail descends a steep series of switchbacks down Hualapai Canyon to the juncture with Havasu Canyon. This one critical turn is marked with a sign pointing the way to Supai. The climate change is dramatic at this point where the sunburned cliffs and parched desert terrain give way to the lush greenery lining the twisting, turquoise course of Havasu Creek.

8 MI: SUPAI

You'll see irrigation ditches and patches of farmland as you near the pastoral village of Supai. Two red-stone sentinels stand guard over the village. Legend claims that if they should ever fall, the canyon walls will close and the village will be destroyed. The trail widens into a sandy lane as it enters the village. All visitors need to check in with the tourist office, located in the center of town.

9.5 MI: NAVAJO FALLS

The trail narrows as it leaves the village. The first of the three major waterfalls, Navajo Falls, drops 75 feet over a travertine encrusted cliff. The trail passes to the right of the waterfall.

10 MI: HAVASU FALLS

The canyon narrows as it approaches Havasu Falls, where the creek dashes through a notch in the Redwall Limestone before dramatically dropping 100 feet into a glittering blue-green pool—the most popular swimming hole along the way. The trail, constructed by the Civilian Conservation Corps in the 1930s, descends along the west side of the waterfall.

11 MI: MOONEY FALLS

Havasu Campground stretches along the banks of the creek at the top of Mooney Falls, the tallest of the waterfalls. This spectacularly singular waterfall plummets 196 feet into a deep, azure pool below. Take care along the steep descent to the canyon floor. Mist, billowing out from the base of the waterfall, makes the footing slippery, but a chain railing offers some extra security.

HAVASU TRAIL TIPS

- Visitation into the canyon is limited. Hikers must obtain advance approval to enter the reservation and must pay a fee of $35 per person (plus an additional "environmental" fee of $5 per person, refundable if you carry out a bag of trash back to Hualapai Hilltop). Once in Havasu Canyon, hikers must pay $17 per person per night to camp, or hikers can stay at Havasupai Lodge.

- Pack adequate food and supplies. There's no water (or gas for that matter) available at the Havasu Hilltop Trailhead, though some vendors may be selling snacks and water there. Prices for food and sundry items in Supai are more than double what they would be outside of the reservation.

- Alcohol, drugs, weapons, pets, and nude swimming are prohibited.

- Hikers must stay on established trails.

SUMMER SPORTS & ACTIVITIES

AIR TOURS

Helicopter tours are offered by Heli USA at Grand Canyon West and are also included in the Journey package offered by Destination Grand Canyon. Airwest Helicopters runs regular service for those staying at Hualapai Lodge.

OUTFITTERS

Airwest Helicopters (☎623/516–2790)offers rides into Havasu Canyon to those staying at Hualapai Lodge. Flights leave from Hualapai Hilltop and cost $85 per person each way. They do not accept reservations and visitors are transported on a first-come, first-served basis. Tribal members have priority seating on all flights. From mid-March through mid-October helicopters fly from 10 AM to 1 PM, Monday, Thursday, Friday, and Sunday. Winter flights run from 10 AM to 1 PM on Friday and Sunday. ✉Havasupai Tourist Enterprise, Supai 86435 ☎928/448–2141 or 928/448–2121 for general information and camping/hiking reservations, 928/448–2111 or 928/448–2201 for lodging reservations ⊕www.havasupaitribe.com 🛏 $35 per person entrance fee, $5 per person environmental-care fee.

Grand Canyon West Ranch. Get aerial views of the Colorado River, canyon cliffs, and rock formations at Grand Canyon West with Heli USA's "To the Edge and Beyond" helicopter tour. ✉*Grand Canyon* ☎*702/736–8787 or 800/359–8727* ⊕*www.grandcanyonranch.com* ⊕*$119.*

HORSEBACK RIDING

See the remote countryside on horseback with guided rides offered by working cowboys at Grand Canyon West Ranch and by riders on the West Rim at Hualapai Ranch. In Havasu Canyon, Havasupai Tourist Enterprises offers horseback rides from Hualapai Hilltop to Supai.

OUTFITTERS

Destination Grand Canyon. Take a horseback ride to Quartermaster Point with Indian cowboy guides. Horseback rides leave from Hualapai Ranch. The ranch offers 30-minute rides for $59 and 90-minute rides for $79. ✉*Grand Canyon West* ☎*702/878–9378 or 877/716–9378* ⊕*www. destinationgrandcanyon.com* ⊕*$59–$79* ▤*AE, D, MC, V* ⚓*Reservations essential.*

☾ **Grand Canyon West Ranch.** Take a ride on the wild side and explore the oldest working cattle ranch in Mojave County. Half-hour rides cost $39 and one-hour sunset rides cost $55. Riders must be 7 or older. ☎*702/736–8787 or 800/ 359–8727* ⊕*www.grandcanyonranch.com.*

Havasupai Tourist Enterprise. Why walk when you can ride? For a more relaxed approach to Supai, reserve a horse for the 8-mi trek into Havasu Canyon. Round-trip rides from Hualapai Hilltop to the campground are $150 per person, one-way $75. Round-trip rides from Hualapai Hilltop to the lodge are $120 person, one-way $70. Baggage is transported separately by pack mule. Riders must be at least 4-feet, 7-inches tall, weigh less than 250 pounds, and be in fairly good physical condition. Children under 5 may ride double with an adult. Advance reservations are required at least six weeks in advance, and you must make a 50% deposit at the time you make your reservation. Riders are urged to confirm horse reservations the day prior to travel. ☎*928/448–2121, 928/448–2141, 928/448–2174, or 928/448–2180* ⊕*www.havasupaitribe.com.*

JEEP TOURS

Explore the back country with a jeep tour down Diamond Creek Road, the only point other than Lees Ferry accessible by automobile. On the West Rim, Destination Grand Canyon offers half-hour and one-hour Hummer tours, which can be included as an option in the Journey package or purchased separately.

OUTFITTERS

Destination Grand Canyon. Travel off the beaten path with a Hummer adventure offering exclusive views of Grand Canyon West. ✉ *Grand Canyon West* ☎ *702/878–9378 or 877/716–9378* ⊕ *www.destinationgrandcanyon.com* 🛏 *$59–$89* ▭ *AE, D, MC, V* ⚓ *Reservations essential.*

Grand Canyon Old West Jeep Tours. Departing from several locations, these combination tours take adventurous travelers on a Jeep ride down Diamond Creek road to the Colorado River on the Hualapai Indian Reservation. Other aspects of the trip include lunch at the river's edge, photo opportunities, hiking, and a visit to the nearby Grand Canyon Caverns. The rides are bumpy and are not recommended for people with back injuries. ✉ *Grand Canyon* ☎ *928/638–2000 or 866/638–4386* ⊕ *www.grandcanyon jeeps.com* 🛏 *$217–$256* ▭ *AE, D, MC, V* ⚓ *Reservations essential.*

RAFTING

★ FodorsChoice The Hualapai tribe offers one-day white-water trips on the Colorado River.

OUTFITTERS

One-day river trips are offered by the Hualapai tribe through the **Hualapai River Runners** (✉ *887 Rte. 66, Peach Springs 86434* ☎ *928/769–2230 or 888/255–9550* ⊕ *www. destinationgrandcanyon.com*) from March through October. The trips, which cost $350.96 paid in advance, leave from the Hualapai Lodge at 7:30 AM and return between 6:30 and 8:30 PM. The white-water adventure also includes a moderate hike to Travertine Falls. Lunch, snacks, and beverages are provided. Children must be 8 or older to take the trip, which runs several rapids with the most difficult rated as Class V or VI, depending on the river flow.

SIGHTSEEING TOURS

More than 30 tour and transportation companies service Grand Canyon West from Las Vegas by airplane, helicopter, coach, SUV, and Hummer.

OUTFITTERS

Companies worth noting are **Air Vegas** (☎800/940–2550 ⊕*www.airvegas.com*), **Best Las Vegas Tours** (☎866/688–2378 ⊕*www.bestlasvegastours.com*), **Grand Canyon Tour Company** (☎800/2–CANYON ⊕*www.grandcanyontourcompany.com*), **Papillon Grand Canyon Helicopters** (☎928/638–2419 or 800/528–2418 ⊕*www.papillon.com*), **Scenic Airlines** (☎800/634–6801 ⊕*www.scenic.com*), **Vegas Tours** (☎866/218–6877 ⊕*www.vegastours.com*), and **Vision Holidays** (☎800/256–8767 ⊕*www.visionholidays.com*).

EDUCATIONAL PROGRAMS

Over the last several years, the Hualapai Tribe has developed three viewpoints on the far western rim of the Grand Canyon. Local Hualapai guides at all West Rim attractions add a Native American perspective to a canyon trip that you won't find on North and South Rim tours in Grand Canyon National Park.

♺ **Grand Canyon West.** Depending on the package (starting at $30), Hualapai guides will take you to attractions including Eagle Point, where the Indian Village walking tour visits authentic dwellings of the Hualapai, Havasupai, Navajo, Plains, and Hopi; Hualapai Ranch, site of Western performances, cookouts, and horseback and wagon rides; and Guano Point, where the "High Point Hike" offers panoramic views of the Colorado River. ☎702/878–9378, 877/716–9378 ⊕*www.destinationgrandcanyon.com*.

ARTS & ENTERTAINMENT

The annual **Havasupai Peach Festival** (☎928/448–2141 ⊕*www.havasupaitribe.com*) features tribal song and dance, traditional games, and a rodeo during the second weekend of August.

Lodging & Dining in the Park

WORD OF MOUTH

"Stay in the park. Unlike some other National Parks (Grand Teton, Yellowstone, for example) the lodging outside the park is a longer drive. Nothing like rolling out of bed to see sunrise at [the] Canyon or watching sun set."

—gail

By Carrie
Miner

ALTHOUGH NATIVE AMERICANS HAVE BEEN living in and around the Grand Canyon for thousands of years, it wasn't until the 1880s that the first Anglo settlers set up camp at this geological wonder. The harsh Bright Angel Camp opened to visitors in the 1890s (Bright Angel Lodge wasn't added until 1935), but rough terrain and the rigorous demands of stagecoach travel kept visitors to a minimum. It wasn't until the 64-mi railroad from Williams reached the Grand Canyon in 1901 that business on the South Rim boomed. The Santa Fe Railroad commissioned Charles Whittlesey to design El Tovar Hotel, an art-and-crafts masterpiece constructed out of Oregon pine and local stone. Constructed at a then-exorbitant cost of $250,000, this chalet-style hotel offered comfortable rooms and elegant dining to an ever-increasing number of visitors. In 1922, Phantom Ranch opened as the only accommodation on the canyon floor. Famed architect Mary Jane Colter designed Bright Angel Lodge in 1935, intended to provide moderately priced rooms for South Rim visitors.

Due to national-park-construction restrictions, no new lodging developments have been built on either rim since the late 1960s. However, with the continued growth of visitation, limited lodging quickly became problematic. To the south, a strip of hotels catering to Grand Canyon visitors sprang up along the highway in Tusayan. More visitors began staying as far away as Williams, relying on tour operators for transportation to and from the South Rim.

On the North Rim, the Grand Canyon Lodge and its adjacent cabins were originally built in 1927. However, the main lodge burned down in 1932 and was rebuilt in 1936–1937 with the original stone foundation. Built from native stone and timber, the new and improved rustic lodge was constructed with the additions of a sunroom, open terraces, and a large observation deck. Due to extreme winter weather and the small number of year-round residents in outlying areas near the North Rim, lodging remains limited to the Grand Canyon Lodge to this day.

To the west, the Hualapai and the Havasupai Indians continue to thrive as some of the earliest inhabitants of the Grand Canyon. The Hualapai live on a million acres of forested land on the West Rim. In recent years the Hualapai have been expanding tourist offerings including lodging at the tribal capital of Peach Springs and at the remote West Rim. The Havasupai, which only number about 600 members, are one of the most isolated Indian tribes in the Southwest. They live in Havasu Canyon, a 188,077-acre reservation surrounded by national-park lands. The cascading blue-green waterfalls in the canyon are a popular destination, but the tribe continue to carefully limit tourism within their homelands.

WHERE TO EAT

Inside Grand Canyon National Park, you can find everything from cafeteria food to casual café fare to elegant evening specials. There's even a coffeehouse brewing organic joe. Reservations are accepted (and recommended) only at El Tovar Dining Room; they can be made 6 months in advance with El Tovar room reservations, 30 days in advance without. The dress code is casual across the board, but El Tovar is your best option if you're looking to dress up a bit and thumb through an extensive wine list. On the North Rim there is just one restaurant: the Grand Canyon Lodge Dining Room. Reservations here are absolutely essential.

If you decide to dine alfresco, be aware that drinking water and restrooms are not available at most picnic spots. However, there are restrooms at the South Kaibab Trailhead picnic area on the South Rim and at the picnic areas at Point Imperial and Cape Royal on the North Rim. Options outside the park, in Tusayan and Williams to the south and Jacob Lake to the north, range from fast food to nice sit-down restaurants. Near the park, even the priciest places allow casual dress. On the Hualapai and Havasupai Reservations in Havasu Canyon and on the West Rim, dining is limited to the restaurants run by the tribes.

WHAT IT COSTS				
¢	$	$$	$$$	$$$$
RESTAURANTS				
under $8	$8–$12	$13–$20	$21–$30	over $30

Restaurant prices are per person for a main course at dinner and do not include any service charges or taxes.

SOUTH RIM

$$$–$$$$ ✕**Phantom Ranch Canteen.** The only eating establishment beneath the canyon rim within the National Park boundaries, this popular mess hall serves up scheduled meals for breakfast, lunch, and dinner. There are two scheduled breakfast times and two scheduled evening menu plans (one dishing up a steak dinner and the other offering your choice of a hearty stew or a vegetarian chili). Sack lunches are available for pick-up at any time. Hikers must reserve meals separately and as far in advance as possible (up to 13 months ahead). ⊠*Phantom Ranch, on canyon floor, at intersection of the Bright Angel and Kaibab trails, Box 699, 86023* ☎*928/638–2631* ⊕*www.grandcanyonlodges. com* ⌂*Reservations essential* ▭*AE, D, DC, MC, V.*

★ **Fodor'sChoice** ✕**El Tovar Dining Room.** No doubt about it—this
$$–$$$$ is the best restaurant for miles. Modeled after a European hunting lodge, breakfast, lunch, and dinner are served beneath the beamed ceiling of a rustic 19th-century dining room built of hand-hewn logs. The cuisine is modern Southwestern with an exotic flair. Start with the hoisin-barbecue sea scallops or the mozzarella roulades of prosciutto and basil pesto—both are divine. The dinner menu includes such dishes as mesquite-smoked pork chops with wild-rice stuffing, grilled New York strip steak with buttermilk-cornmeal onion rings, and a salmon tostada topped with organic greens and tequila vinaigrette. Half portions are available for children under 12. The dining room also offers an extensive wine list suitable for a wide range of palettes. Dinner reservations can be made up to 6 months in advance with room reservations and 30 days in advance for all other visitors. ⊠*El Tovar Hotel, Grand Canyon Village, Box 699, 86023* ☎*303/297–2757 or 888/297–2757 (reservations only), 928/638–2631 Ext. 6432* ⊕*www. grandcanyonlodges.com* ⌂*Reservations essential* ▭*AE, D, DC, MC, V* ⊘*Closed daily 2–5.*

$$–$$$ ✕**Arizona Room.** The canyon views from this casual Southwestern-style steak house are the best of any restaurant at the South Rim. The menu includes such delicacies as chili-crusted pan-seared wild salmon, chipotle-barbecue baby-back ribs, roasted-vegetable and black-bean enchiladas, and mustard- and rosemary-crusted prime rib. For dessert, try the cheesecake with prickly pear syrup paired with one of the house's specialty coffee drinks. Seating is first-come, first-served, so arrive early to avoid the crowds. ⊠*Bright*

Angel Lodge, Grand Canyon Village, Box 699, 86023 ☎928/638–2631 ⊕*www.grandcanyonlodges.com* ⚲*Reservations not accepted* ⊟*AE, D, DC, MC, V* ⊘*Closed Jan.–mid-Feb. No lunch Nov.–Feb.*

$–$$ ✕**Bright Angel Restaurant.** The draw here is casual, affordable dining. No-surprises dishes will fill your belly at breakfast, lunch, or dinner. Entrées include such basics as salads, steaks, pasta, fajitas, and fish. The dining room bustles all day long. The plain decor is broken up with large pane windows and original artwork. ■**TIP→Don't wait until the last minute to use the restroom: you have to leave the restaurant, and walk through the lobby and down a flight of stairs to get there—where you'll most likely need to wait in line with all of the other canyon visitors.** ⊠*Bright Angel Lodge, Grand Canyon Village, Box 699, 86023* ☎928/638–2631 ⊕*www. grandcanyonlodges.com* ⚲*Reservations not accepted* ⊟*AE, D, DC, MC, V.*

¢–$ ✕**Bright Angel Fountain.** This is the place on the rim to stop for a quick bite or a scoop (or two) of ice cream. The fountain is open seasonally weather permitting. ⊠*Bright Angel Lodge, Grand Canyon Village, Box 699, 86023* ☎928/638–2631 ⊕*www.grandcanyonlodges.com* ⊘*Closed Oct.–Apr. No dinner.*

¢–$ ✕**Desert View Trading Post Cafeteria.** This self-service cafeteria serves up pastries, salads, sandwiches, pizza, and more for breakfast, lunch, and dinner. ⊠*Desert View Trading Post, Desert View Dr., Box 699, 86023* ☎928/638–2631 ⊕*www.grandcanyonlodges.com* ⊟*AE, D, DC, MC, V* ⊘*No dinner mid-Oct.–mid-May.*

¢–$ ✕**Maswik Cafeteria.** You can pick up a burger, pasta, or affordable Mexican fare at this family-friendly food court. ⊠*Maswik Lodge, Grand Canyon Village, Box 699, 86023* ☎928/638–2631 ⊕*www.grandcanyonlodges.com* ⚲*Reservations not accepted* ⊟*AE, D, DC, MC, V.*

¢ ✕**Canyon Coffee House.** The Bright Angel Lounge doubles as this popular coffee shop in the early morning hours. Pair an espresso, cappuccino, or a latte with your choice of fruit, scones, croissants, muffins, or bagels for a quick and easy start to any day. ⊠*Bright Angel Lodge, Grand Canyon Village, Box 699, 86023* ☎928/638–2631 ⊕*www. grandcanyonlodges.com* ⊘*No lunch or dinner.*

¢ ✕**Hermits Rest Snack Bar.** This is the place to stop on Hermit Road for a quick beverage, pastry, or sandwich. The snack bar closes at sunset. ⊠*Hermits Rest, 7 mi west of Grand Canyon Village, Box 699, 86023* ☎*928/638–2351* ⊕*www. grandcanyonlodges.com.*

¢ ✕**Yavapai Canyon Café.** Fast-food favorites here include fried chicken, chicken potpie, and fried catfish; there's also a salad bar. Open for breakfast, lunch, and dinner, the cafeteria also serves specials. ⊠*Yavapai Lodge, Grand Canyon Village, Box 699, 86023* ☎*928/638–2631* ⚠*Reservations not accepted* ═*AE, D, DC, MC, V* ⊘*Closed mid-Dec.–Feb.*

PICNIC AREAS

Buggeln. This secluded, shady area is wheelchair accessible, with assistance. ⊠*15 mi east of Grand Canyon Village on Desert View Dr.*

South Kaibab Trailhead. This picnic area is the closest to the park's hub; it is often filled with hikers' cars. ⊠*On Desert View Dr., 1 mi east of Grand Canyon Village.*

NORTH RIM

$$–$$$ ✕**Grand Canyon Lodge Dining Room.** The historic lodge has
★ a huge, high-ceilinged dining room with spectacular views and very good food; you might find pork medallions, roast chicken, and buffalo steaks on the dinner menu. The dining room is closed from 10 to 11:30 am and from 2:30 to 4:45 pm. ⊠*Grand Canyon Lodge, Bright Angel Point, 86052* ☎*877/386–4383 ext. 760* ⚠*Reservations not accepted* ═*AE, D, DC, MC, V* ⊘*Closed mid-Oct.–mid-May.*

¢ ✕**Deli in the Pines.** Dining choices are very limited on the North Rim, but this is your best bet for a meal on a budget. Selections include pizza, salads, deli sandwiches, hot dogs, rice bowls, and ice cream. Open for breakfast, lunch, and dinner. ⊠*Grand Canyon Lodge, Bright Angel Point, 86052* ☎*877/386–4383* ⚠*Reservations not accepted* ═*AE, D, DC, MC, V* ⊘*Closed mid-Oct. to mid-May.*

¢ ✕**Roughrider Saloon.** From 5:30 to 10:30 AM this pub doubles as a coffeehouse serving up gourmet coffee and assorted pastries. A grouping of tables in front of a large window has a view of the busy boardwalk. Head to the cozy couch in the corner for some peace and quiet. ⊠*Grand Canyon Lodge, Bright Angel Point, 86052* ☎*8778/386–4383* ═*AE, D, DC, MC, V* ⊘*Closed mid-Oct.–mid-May.*

PICNIC AREAS

★ **Cape Royal.** This is the most popular designated picnic area on the North Rim because of its panoramic views. ⊠ *23 mi south of North Rim Visitor Center.*

Point Imperial. If you're looking for privacy, head here, where the shade shelters you. ⊠ *11 mi northeast of the North Rim Visitor Center.*

WEST RIM

$$ ✕ **Diamond Creek Restaurant.** Located in the Hualapai Lodge at Peach Springs, this casual eatery serves up American standards—hamburgers, barbecue ribs, ribeye steak, and baked chicken—as well as ethnic specialties, including Hualapai stew and a Hualapai taco, plate-sized pieces of fried bread smothered with beans, meat, lettuce, cheese, and salsa. ⊠ *900 Rte. 66, Peach Springs 86434* ☎ *928/769–2230 or 888/255–9550* ⊕ *www.destinationgrandcanyon. com* ═ *AE, D, MC, V.*

WHERE TO STAY

The park's accommodations include three "historic rustic" facilities and four motel-style lodges. Of the 922 rooms, cabins, and suites, only 203, all at the Grand Canyon Lodge, are located at the North Rim. Outside of El Tovar Hotel, the canyon's architectural crown jewel, frills are hard to find. Rooms are basic but comfortable, and most guests would agree that the best in-room amenity is a view of the canyon. Though rates vary widely, most rooms fall in the $125 to $136 range.

Reservations are a must, especially during the busy summer season. If you want to get your first choice (especially Bright Angel Lodge or El Tovar), make reservations as far in advance as possible; they're taken up to 13 months ahead. You might find a last-minute cancellation, but you shouldn't count on it. Although lodging at the South Rim will keep you close to the action, the frenetic activity and crowded facilities are off-putting to some. With short notice, the best time to find a room on the South Rim is during winter. And though the North Rim is less crowded than the South Rim, lodging (remember that rooms are limited) is available only from mid-May through mid-October.

Outside the park, Tusayan's hotels offer a convenient location but no bargains, whereas Williams and Flagstaff can provide price breaks on food and lodging, as well as a respite from the crowds. Extra amenities (e.g., swimming pools and Internet access) are also more abundant. Reservations are always a good idea.

Lodging options are even more limited on the West Rim. The Hualapai Lodge in Peach Springs and the Hualapai Ranch at Grand Canyon West are run by the Hualapai tribe. The Havasupai Lodge in Supai offers the only rooms in Havasu Canyon.

WHAT IT COSTS				
¢	$	$$	$$$	$$$$
HOTELS				
under $70	$70–$120	$121–$175	$176–$250	over $250

Hotel prices are for a double room in high season and do not include taxes, service charges, or resort fees

SOUTH RIM

★ Fodor's Choice
$$–$$$$

☒ El Tovar Hotel. A registered National Historic Landmark, El Tovar was built in 1905 of Oregon pine logs and native stone. Also known as the "Crown Jewel" of the South Rim, El Tovar has hosted such dignitaries as Theodore Roosevelt and Albert Einstein. The hotel's proximity to all of the canyon's facilities, its European hunting-lodge atmosphere, and its renowned dining room make it the best place to stay on the South Rim. It's usually booked well in advance (up to 13 months ahead), though it's easier to get a room during winter months. Three suites (El Tovar, Fred Harvey, and Mary Jane Colter) and several rooms have canyon views (these are booked up as early as a year in advance), but you can enjoy the view anytime from the cocktail-lounge back porch. **Pros:** Historic lodging located just steps from the South Rim; fabulous lounge with outdoor seating and canyon views; best in-park dining located on-site in the El Tovar Dining Room. **Cons:** Books up quickly; no Internet access. ☒ *Grand Canyon Village ☐ Box 699, Grand Canyon 86023 ☎303/297–2757 or 888/297–2757 (reservations only), 928/638–2631 ☎303/297–3175 (reservations only) ⊕www.grandcanyon lodges.com ➪66 rooms, 12 suites ♿In-room: refrigerator.*

In-hotel: restaurant, room service, bar, no-smoking rooms ⊟*AE, D, DC, MC, V.*

$$ ⊡Kachina Lodge. Located on the rim halfway between El Tovar and Bright Angel Lodge, this motel-style lodge has many rooms with partial canyon views ($10 extra). Although lacking the historical charm of the neighboring lodges, these rooms are a good bet for families and are within easy walking distance of dining facilities at El Tovar and Bright Angel Lodge. There are also several rooms for people with physical disabilities. There's no air-conditioning, but evaporative coolers keep the heat at bay. Check-in at El Tovar Hotel to the east. Kids under 16 stay free. **Pros:** Partial canyon views in some rooms; family-friendly; handicap accessible rooms. **Cons:** No Internet access; check-in takes place at El Tovar Hotel; limited parking. ⊠*Grand Canyon Village,* ⊕*Box 699, Grand Canyon 86023* ☎*303/297–2757 or 888/297–2757 (reservations only),* *928/638–2631* ⊟*303/297–3175 (reservations only)* ⊕*www.grandcanyonlodges.com* ⌖*49 rooms* ⌂*In-room: safe, refrigerator, Ethernet, no a/c. In-hotel: no-smoking rooms* ⊟*AE, D, DC, MC, V.*

$$ ⊡Thunderbird Lodge. This motel with comfortable, no-nonsense rooms is next to Bright Angel Lodge in Grand Canyon Village. For $10 more, you can get a room with a partial view of the canyon. Rooms have either two queen beds or one king. Check-in at Bright Angel Lodge, the next hotel to the west. Some rooms do not have air-conditioning, but instead have evaporative coolers. Kids under 16 stay free. **Pros:** Partial canyon views in some rooms; family-friendly; handicap-accessible rooms. **Cons:** No Internet access; check-in takes place at Bright Angel Lodge; limited parking. ⊠*Grand Canyon Village,* ⊕*Box 699, Grand Canyon 86023* ☎*303/297–2757 or 888/297–2757 (reservations only),* *928/638–2631* ⊟*303/297–3175 (reservations only)* ⊕*www.grandcanyonlodges.com* ⌖*55 rooms* ⌂*In-room: no a/c (some), safe, refrigerator. In-hotel: no-smoking rooms* ⊟*AE, D, DC, MC, V.*

$–$$ ⊡Bright Angel Lodge. Famed architect Mary Jane Colter ☾ designed this 1935 log-and-stone structure, which sits within a few yards of the canyon rim and blends superbly with the canyon walls. It offers a similar location to El Tovar for about half the price. Accommodations are in motel-style rooms or cabins. Lodge rooms don't have TVs, and some rooms do not have private bathrooms. Scattered among the pines are 50 cabins, which do have TVs and private baths; some have fireplaces. Expect historic charm but not luxury. The Bright Angel Dining Room serves family-style meals all day and a warm apple-grunt dessert large enough to share. The Arizona Room serves dinner only. Adding to the experience are an ice-cream parlor, gift shop, and small history museum with exhibits on Fred Harvey and Mary Jane Colter. **Pros:** Some rooms have canyon views and all are steps away from the rim; Internet kiosks in the lobby; transportation desk for the mule ride check-in is located in the lobby. **Cons:** The popular lodge is always packed; parking here is problematic; stairs throughout the building and lack of elevators make handicap accessibility an issue. ⊠*Grand Canyon Village* ⌕*Box 699, Grand Canyon 86023* ☎*303/297–2757, 888/297–2757 (reservations only), 928/638–2631* ⊟*303/297–3175 (reservations only)* ⊕*www.grandcanyonlodges.com* ⇦*37 rooms, 6 with shared toilet and shower, 13 with shared shower; 50 cabins* ♿*In-room: no a/c, no TV (some). In-hotel: restaurant, bar, public Internet* ⊟*AE, D, DC, MC, V.*

$–$$ ▦**Maswik Lodge.** The lodge, named for a Hopi Kachina ☾ who is said to guard the canyon, is ¼ mi from the rim. Accommodations, nestled in the ponderosa-pine forest, range from rustic cabins to more modern rooms, refurbished in 2006. The cabins are the cheapest option but are available only spring through fall. Some rooms have air-conditioning, and the rest have ceiling fans. Maswik Cafeteria offers sandwiches, salads, snack foods, and a choice of several hot meals. Teenagers like the lounge, where they can shoot pool, throw darts, or watch the big-screen TV. Kids under 16 stay free. **Pros:** Has larger rooms than historic lodgings, which are good for families; Internet access; affordable dining options. **Cons:** Plain rooms lack historic charm; lodge is tucked away from the rim in the forest. ⊠*Grand Canyon Village* ⌕*Box 699, Grand Canyon 86023* ☎*303/297–2757 or 888/297–2757 (reservations only), 928/638–2631* ⊟*303/297–3175 (reservations only)* ⊕*www.grandcanyonlodges.com* ⇦*250 rooms, 28 cabins* ♿*In-room: no a/c (some). In-hotel: 2 restaurants, public Internet, no-smoking rooms* ⊟*AE, D, DC, MC, V.*

$–$$ ▦**Yavapai Lodge.** The largest motel-style lodge in the park is tucked in a piñon and juniper forest at the eastern end of Grand Canyon Village, near the RV park. The basic rooms are near the park's general store, the visitor center (½ mi), and the rim (¼ mi). The cafeteria, open for breakfast, lunch, and dinner, serves standard park-service food. An Internet room is available to guests. **Pros:** Transportation/ activities desk on-site in the lobby; located near Market Plaza in Grand Canyon Village; forested grounds offer plenty of room for kids to run. **Cons:** Cafeteria meals are unexciting; farthest in-park lodging from the rim. ✉*Grand Canyon Village* ⓓ*Box 699, Grand Canyon 86023* ☎*303/297–2757 or 888/297–2757 (reservations only), 928/638–2631* ⎙*303/297–3175 (reservations only)* ⊕*www.grandcanyonlodges.com* ⤏*358 rooms* ⑁*In-room: refrigerator. In-hotel: restaurant, public Internet, no-smoking rooms* ⊟*AE, D, DC, MC, V* ⊘*Closed Jan. and Feb.*

¢ 🔟**Phantom Ranch.** In a grove of cottonwood trees on the canyon floor, Phantom Ranch is accessible only to hikers and mule trekkers. The wood-and-stone buildings originally made up a hunting camp built in 1922. There are 40 dormitory beds and 14 beds in cabins, all with shared baths. Seven additional cabins are reserved for mule riders, who buy their trips as a package. The mess hall–style restaurant, one of the most remote eating establishments in the United States, serves family-style meals, with breakfast, dinner, and box lunches available. Hikers looking to lighten their load can also take advantage of the ranch's duffel service: bags or packs weighing 30 pounds or less can be transported to the ranch by mule for a fee of $60 each way. Reservations for all services, taken up to 13 months in advance, are a must. **Pros:** Only inner-canyon lodging option; fabulous canyon views; remote access limits crowds. **Cons:** Accessible only by foot or mule; no television, phones, or air-conditioning. ✉*On canyon floor, at intersection of the Bright Angel and Kaibab trails, Box 699, 86023* ☎*303/297–2757 or 888/297–2757* ⎙*303/297–3175 (reservations only)* ⊕*www.grandcanyonlodges.com* ⤏*4 dormitories and 2 cabins for hikers, 7 cabins with outside showers for mule riders* ⑁*In-room: no a/c, no phone, no TV. In-hotel: restaurant* ⊟*AE, D, DC, MC, V.*

NORTH RIM

★ **Fodor's**Choice 🔟**Grand Canyon Lodge.** This historic property,
$–$$ constructed mainly in the 1920s and '30s, is the premier lodging facility in the North Rim area. The main building has limestone walls and timbered ceilings. Lodging options include small, rustic cabins; larger cabins (some with a canyon view and some with two bedrooms); and newer, tradi-

tional motel rooms. The best of the bunch are log cabins 301 and 306, which have private porches perched on the lip of the canyon. Other cabins with fabulous canyon views include 305, 309, and 310. You might find marinated-pork kebabs or linguine with cilantro on the dining room's dinner menu ($–$$$). Dining-room reservations are essential and should be made as far in advance as possible. **Pros:** Steps away from gorgeous North Rim views; close to several easy hiking trails. **Cons:** As the only in-park lodging option, this lodge fills up fast; no televisions or a/c; no Internet access. ✉*Hwy. 67, North Rim, Grand Canyon National Park 86052* ☎*877/386–4383 or 928/638–2611 (May–Oct.); 928/645–6865 (Nov.—Apr.)*☎*480/998–7399 (reservations only)* ⊕*www.grandcanyonforever.com* ☞*44 rooms, 157 cabins* ⚿*In-room: no a/c, no TV. In-hotel: 3 restaurants, bar, laundry facilities, public internet, no-smoking rooms* ▭*AE, D, MC, V* ⊗*Closed mid-Oct.–mid-May.* .

WEST RIM & HAVASU CANYON

$$ ✕▥**Havasupai Lodge.** These are fairly spartan accommodations, but you won't mind much when you see the natural beauty surrounding you. The lodge and restaurant are at the bottom of Havasu Canyon and are operated by the Havasupai tribe. The restaurant serves three meals a day, mostly sandwiches and fast-food-type fare, and a daily special ($). In addition to the room rate, there is a $35 per-person tribal-entry fee. Reservations are essential and can be made up to a year in advance. **Pros:** Located near the famous waterfalls; Havasupai staff offers a Native American perspective on the natural and cultural history of the Grand Canyon experience. **Cons:** Accessible only by foot, horseback, or helicopter; rooms are plain and worn; no phones or TVs. ✉*Box 160, Supai 86435* ☎*928/448–2111 or 928/448–2201* ⊕*www.havasupaitribe.com* ☞*24 rooms* ⚿*In-room: no phone, no TV. In-hotel: restaurant, no-smoking rooms* ▭*MC, V.*

$$ ✕▥**Hualapai Ranch.** Cabins are clean and neat, but also very small and unassuming. You won't be tempted to spend a lot of time in your rooms, but the front porches make for a good place to sit and unwind after a hectic day exploring the sights at the West Rim. The cabins are adjacent to a small "Western" town, where visitors can pose for snapshots, sign up for guided horseback tours and wagon

rides, watch gunfight re-enactments in the dusty streets, visit a petting zoo, join a sing-along at the evening campfire programs, and sit down for a barbecue dinner in the dining room. The Tranquility package (one night) and the Serenity package (two nights) include three meals a day, a Hualapai visitation permit, and motor-coach transfers to the rim, which overlooks Guano Point and Eagle Point. **Pros:** Front porches offer relaxed desert views; rustlers tell tall tales and strike up a tune at campfire programs; dining room serves meals all day. **Cons:** No Internet access; no phones or TVs. ☏*6206 W. Desert Inn, Ste. B, Las Vegas 89146* ☎*702/878–9378 or 889/878–9378* ⊕*www.destina tiongrandcanyon.com* ⟟*20 cabins* ⟐*In-room: no phone, no TV. In-hotel: restaurant* ⊟*AE, MC, V.*

$ ⊞**Grand Canyon West Ranch.** Sprawling at the base of Spirit Mountain, this historic 106,000-acre working cattle ranch takes guests on an adventure to the Old West. Corriente cattle still roam the hills and their cowboy caretakers lead guided horseback tours and horse-drawn wagon rides through the rugged countryside. Louis L'Amour and Andy Devine supposedly spent some time working at this ranch, which has been moving cattle for more than 150 years. Located 14 mi southwest of the Grand Canyon West Airport on Diamond Bar Road, the ranch offers a kitschy collection of Indian tipis and pine cabins for folks looking for lodging in this remote region. Helicopter tours into the canyon, evening campfire programs, and adult beverages at the Diamond Bar add to the Western-themed attraction. Room rates include three meals a day. **Pros:** Closest lounge to Grand Canyon West; lodging is all-inclusive. **Cons:** Located 25 minutes from Grand Canyon West activities; no Internet access; no phones or TVs. ☒*3750 E. Diamond Bar Rd., Meadview 86444* ☎*702/736–8787 or 800/359–8727* ☎*702/736 0835* ⊕*www.grandcanyonranch.com* ⟟*10 cabins, 5 tipis* ⟐*In-room: no phone, no TV. In-hotel: restaurant, bar* ⊟*AE, D, DC, MC, V.*

¢–$ ⊞**Hualapai Lodge.** Located at Peach Springs, the hotel has a comfortable lobby with a large fireplace that is welcoming on chilly nights. The rooms are clean but basic. The Diamond Creek Restaurant offers standard American fare, including hamburgers and sandwiches, along with specialties such as Hualapai tacos, which are worth a stop on their own. The activities desk in lobby arranges tours to Grand Canyon West. **Pros:** Saltwater pool; on-site restaurant mixes things up with Native American dishes;

5

Hualapai locals add a Native American perspective to the Grand Canyon experience. **Cons:** Basic rooms lack historic charm; no Internet access. ✉*900 Rte. 66, Peach Springs 86434* ☎*928/769–2230 or 888/255–9550* ⊕*www.destinationgrandcanyon.com* ⇆*57 rooms* ⚲*In-hotel: restaurant, pool, gym, spa, laundry facilities, no-smoking rooms* ▭*AE, MC, V.*

WHERE TO CAMP

Inside the park, camping is permitted only in designated campsites. Some campgrounds charge nightly camping fees in addition to entrance fees, and some accept reservations up to five months in advance. Others are first-come, first-served. The South Rim has three campgrounds, one with RV hookups. The North Rim's single in-park campground does not offer hookups. All four campgrounds are near the rims and easily accessible. In-park camping in a spot other than a developed rim campground requires a permit from the Backcountry Information Center, which also serves as your reservation. Permits can be requested by mail or fax; applying well in advance is recommended. Call 928/638–7875 for information. Numerous backcountry campsites dot the canyon—be prepared for a considerable hike. The three established backcountry campgrounds require a trek of 4.6 to 16.6 mi.

WHAT IT COSTS				
$$$$	$$$	$$	$	¢
CAMPING				
over $25	$21–$25	$15–$20	$8–$14	under $8

Camping prices are for a campsites including a tent area, fire pit, bear-proof food-storage box, picnic table; potable water and pit toilets or restrooms will be nearby.

Outside the park, two campgrounds, one with hookups, are located within 7 mi of the South Rim and two are located within about 45 mi of the North Rim. At this writing, one was closed for renovations; the other has hookups and accepts reservations. Developed and undeveloped campsites are available, first-come, first-served, in the Kaibab National Forest.

There is no camping on the West Rim, but you can pitch a tent on the beach near the Colorado River at the primitive campground on Diamond Creek Road. Hikers heading to the falls in Havasu Canyon can stay at the primitive campground in Supai.

SOUTH RIM

★ Fodor'sChoice ⚠ **Mather Campground.** Mather has RV and tent

$$ sites but no hookups. No reservations are accepted from December to March, but the rest of the year, especially during the busy spring and summer seasons, they are a good idea, and can be made up to five months in advance. Ask at the campground entrance for same-day availability. Senior and Access park-pass holders pay half price. ✉ *Off Village Loop Dr., Grand Canyon Village 86023* ⬦ *Reserve America* ☎ *877/444–6777* ⬦ *www.recreation.gov* ⬦ *308 sites for RVs and tents* ⬦ *Flush toilets, pay phones, drinking water, guest laundry, showers, fire grates, picnic tables, dump station* ⬦ *Open year-round.*

$$ ⚠ **Trailer Village.** This campground in Grand Canyon Village has RV sites—but no tent-camping sites—with full hookups and bathroom facilities, though the bathrooms are ½ mi from the campground. The fee is good for two people, with an extra $2 fee for each additional person over age 16. The facility is very busy during spring and summer, so make reservations ahead of time (not accepted December through March). The dump station is closed in winter. ✉ *Off Village Loop Dr., Grand Canyon Village 86023* ☎ *303/297–2757, 888/297–2757 (reservations only)* ⬦ *303/297–3175 (reservations only)* ⬦ *www.xanterra.com* ⬦ *79 RV sites* ⬦ *Flush toilets, full hookups, dump station, drinking water, guest laundry, showers, fire grates* ⬦ *Open year-round.*

$ ⚠ **Desert View Campground.** Popular for spectacular views of the canyon from the nearby Watchtower, this campground fills up fast in summer. Fifty RV (without hookups) and tent sites are available on a first-come, first-served basis. ✉ *Desert View Dr., 23 mi east of Grand Canyon Village off Hwy. 64* ⬦ *Backcountry Office, Box 129, Grand Canyon 86023* ☎ *928/638–7875* ⬦ *928/638–2125* ⬦ *Grills, flush toilets, drinking water, picnic tables* ⬦ *50 campsites* ⬦ *Reservations not accepted* ⬦ *Mid-May–mid-Oct.*

INNER CANYON

¢ ⚠ **Bright Angel Campground.** This campground is near Phantom Ranch on the South and North Kaibab trails at the bottom of the canyon. There are toilet facilities and running water, but no showers. If you plan to eat at the Phantom Ranch Canteen, make your reservation far in advance. Hikers looking to lighten their load can also take advantage of the ranch's duffel service: bags or packs weighing 30 pounds or less can be transported to the ranch by mule for a fee of $60 each way. Reservations for all services, taken up to 13 months in advance, are a must. A backcountry permit, which serves as your reservation, is required to stay here. ✉*Intersection of South and North Kaibab trails, Grand Canyon* ⚐*Backcountry Office, Box 129, Grand Canyon 86023* ☎*928/638–7875* 📠*928/638–2125* ⚑*31 tent sites, 2 large sites* ⚗*Flush toilets, drinking water, picnic tables* ⚗*Backcountry permit required* ☉*Open year-round.*

¢ ⚠ **Cottonwood Campground.** This is the last canyon camp before you ascend to the North Rim. A backcountry permit, which serves as your reservation, is required to stay here. ✉*On the North Kaibab Trail, 16.6 mi from the South Rim Bright Angel trailhead and 7 mi below the North Rim, Grand Canyon* ⚐*Backcountry Office, Box 129, Grand Canyon 86023* ☎*928/638–7875* 📠*928/638–2125* ⚑*11 tent sites, 1 large site* ⚗*Pit toilets, drinking water available mid-May–mid-Oct., shade trees* ⚗*Backcountry permit required* ☉*Year-round; ranger station closed Nov.–Apr.*

¢ ⚠ **Indian Garden.** Halfway down the canyon is this campground, en route to Phantom Ranch on the Bright Angel Trail. Running water and toilet facilities are available, but not showers. A backcountry permit, which serves as a reservation, is required. ✉*Bright Angel Trail, Grand Canyon* ⚐*Backcountry Office, Box 129, Grand Canyon 86023* ☎*928/638–7875* 📠*928/638–2125* ⚗*Vault toilets, drinking water, picnic tables* ⚑*15 tent sites* ⚗*Reservations essential* ☉*Year-round.*

NORTH RIM

$ ⚠ **North Rim Campground.** The only designated campground at the North Rim of Grand Canyon National Park sits 3 mi north of the rim, and has 83 RV and tent sites (no hookups). You can reserve a site up to five months in advance.

Senior and Access park-pass holders pay half price. ⊠*Hwy. 67, Grand Canyon* ⊕*Reserve America* ☎*877/444–6777* ⊕*www.recreation.gov* ⇴*83 campsites* ⚒*Flush toilets, dump station, drinking water, guest laundry, showers, fire grates, picnic tables, general store* ⚑*Reservations essential* ⊙*Generally open mid-May–mid-Oct., possibly later, weather permitting.*

WEST RIM

$$ Diamond Creek. The Hualapai permit camping on their tribal lands here with an overnight camping permit of $20 per person, per night, which can be purchased at the Hualapai Lodge. You can camp on the beach of the Colorado River, but be aware that you might not be alone. As the only place on the river accessed by road other than Lees Ferry, this smooth beach is a popular with river runners as a launch point and a pullout. The camping area is primitive, with only a picnic table and pit toilets. No fires are allowed, but grills may be used and rock-pit barbecues are available. The campground is open from mid-March through October and is accessed by a 22-mi drive down the gravel Diamond Creek Road. The road can be braved by high-clearance passenger vehicles, but your best bet is one with four-wheel-drive capabilities, especially in the summer when storms are commonplace. ⊠*900 Rte. 66, Peach Springs 86434* ☎*928/769–2230 or 888/255–9550* ⊕*www. destinationgrandcanyon.com* ⇴*57 rooms* ⚒*Pit toilets, picnic tables.*

$ Havasu Canyon. You can stay in the primitive campgrounds in Havasu Canyon for $17 (plus 8% tax) per person, per night, in addition to the $35 per person entry fee. The extensive campground has 100 sites and is located 2 mi from the Supai Village. Cottonwood trees provide plenty of shade and picnic tables can be found near many of the campsites. You can pack in a stove, but no campfires are allowed. ⊠*Box 160, Supai 86435* ☎*928/448–2121, 928/448–2174, 928/448–2180, or 928/448–2140* ⊕*www. havasupaitribe.com* ⚒*Restaurant, general store, pit toilets, drinking water, picnic tables.*

CAMPGROUNDS

Inside the Park	Total # of sites	# of RV sites	# of hook-ups	Drive-to sites	Hike-to sites	Flush toilets	Pit toilets	Drinking water	Showers	Fire grates/pits	Swimming	Boat access	Playground	Dump station	Ranger station	Public telephone	Reservations possible	Daily fee per site	Dates open
Bright Angel	33	0	0		y	y		y									y	Free	Y/R
Cottonwood	12	0	0		y		y	y									y	Free	Y/R
Desert View	50	50	0	y		y	y	y		y					y	y		$12	Mid-May–mid-Oct.
Diamond Creek	57	0	0				y											$20	Mid-Mar.–Oct.
Havasu Canyon	100	0	0		y		y	y									y	$17	Y/R
Indian Garden	15	0	0		y		y	y									y	Free	Y/R
Mather	319	319	0	y	y			y	y	y				y	y	y	y	$18	Y/R
North Rim	83	83	0	y	y			y	y	y				y	y	y	y	$18	May–Oct.
Trailer Village	79	79	79	y	y			y	y	y				y		y	y	$28	Y/R
Near the Park																			
Grand Canyon Camper Village	250	200	200	y	y			y	y	y			y	y	y	y		$3	Y/R
Ten-X Campground	70	0	0	y			y	y										$10–$20	May–Sept.

Y/R = year-round

What's Nearby

WORD OF MOUTH

"From Flagstaff, you can take day trips to Sedona, the Grand Canyon, Petrified Forest/Painted Desert, Meteor Crater, Sunset Crater, and other interesting areas."

—furledleader

By Carrie Miner

DESPITE ITS MAGNIFICENCE, the Grand Canyon remained a well-kept secret until the Santa Fe Railroad built a line from Williams to the South Rim in 1901. A year later, the first automobile arrived at the Grand Canyon after an arduous two-day journey from Flagstaff. In the 1950s, the current highway from Williams was built, and a few years later visitation to the park exceeded 1 million. Today, nearly 5 million people visit the Grand Canyon, and most of these head to the more accessible South Rim.

Just 1 mi south of the entrance station, the tiny community of **Tusayan** offers basic amenities and an airport that serves as a starting point for airplane and helicopter tours of the canyon. Less than 60 mi south on Highway 64, the cozy mountain town of **Williams** lives up to its reputation as the "Gateway to the Grand Canyon." Founded in 1882 when the railroad passed through, it was once a rough-and-tumble joint, replete with saloons and bordellos. Today it reflects a much milder side of the Wild West, with 3,000 residents and 1,512 motel rooms. Wander along main street—part of historic Route 66, but locally named, like the town, after trapper Bill Williams—and indulge in Route 66 nostalgia inside antiques shops or souvenir and T-shirt stores.

Eight miles southeast of Grand Canyon Village on U.S. 180, **Flagstaff** makes a good base for combined explorations of the South Rim and the other natural and cultural wonders on the Colorado Plateau. If you are heading to the Eastern Entrance on the South Rim or to the North Rim via U.S. 89 from Flagstaff, **Cameron** makes a worthwhile stop. You'll find a trading post, gas station, post office, restaurant, and a historic lodge.

Marble Canyon, to the north of Tuba City, marks the geographical beginning of the Grand Canyon at its northeastern tip. It's a good stopping point if you are driving U.S. 89 to the North Rim. En route from the South Rim to the North Rim is **Lees Ferry,** where most of the area's river rafts start their journey. **Fredonia,** a small community of about 1,200, approximately an hour's drive north of the Grand Canyon, is often referred to as the gateway to the North Rim; it's also relatively close to Zion and Bryce Canyon national parks. The tiny town of **Jacob Lake,** nestled high in pine country at an elevation of 7,925 feet, was named after Mormon explorer Jacob Hamblin, also known as the "Buckskin Missionary." Not much more than a lodge and

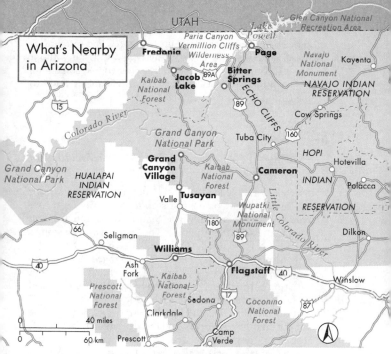

RV park, Jacob Lake is mostly just an en route point for visitors heading to the final 45 mi on Highway 67 to the North Rim.

WHAT IT COSTS				
¢	$	$$	$$$	$$$$
RESTAURANTS				
under $8	$8–$12	$13–$20	$21–$30	over $30
HOTELS				
under $70	$70–$120	$121–$175	$176–$250	over $250

Restaurant prices are per person for a main course at dinner and do not include any service charges or taxes. Hotel prices are for a double room in high season and do not include taxes, service charges, or resort fees

ABOUT THE HOTELS & RESTAURANTS

Don't expect fine dining or fancy hotels in this part of Arizona, but you will find quite a few good local restaurants and many quality hotels and motels to choose from. Flagstaff and Williams have a larger range of dining and lodging choices—including the most upscale hotels and restaurants in the region. If you arrive at the Grand Canyon without any reservations, it's likely you'll be able to find something in one of these two places; of the two, Williams is closer to the Grand Canyon, though Flagstaff is far larger.

TUSAYAN

48 mi north of Williams on AZ 64/U.S. 180, 7 mi south of Grand Canyon Village

Surrounded by federal land, the tiny strip of town known as Tusayan serves as the last stop on Highway 64 before entering the South Entrance Station of Grand Canyon National Park's South Rim. The name Tusayan comes from the Navajo word "Ta-sa-un," which means "a country of isolated buttes." The Spanish changed the name to Tusayan. The private property used to build the current selection of hotels and services was originally homesteaded as farmland and later as a cattle ranch run by the Ten X Cattle Company. In the 1950s, the cattle ranch began selling off the land to developers, the most prominent being R. P. Thurston. In 1963, the Red Feather Lodge was opened, and a year later construction on the Grand Canyon Airport began. In the following decades, new destination lodging continued to develop in an attempt to meet the growing demands for comfortable and affordable accommodations. Today, this small community of 500 residents continues to serve Grand Canyon visitors even though it is limited in growth to the small amount of available private land surrounded by national-forest and park preserves.

WHAT TO SEE

☼ At the **National Geographic Visitor Center Grand Canyon** in Tusayan, discover the canyon's natural history in the 35-minute film *Grand Canyon: The Hidden Secrets,* on an IMAX screen that stands seven stories high. At this popular stop, you can also schedule and purchase tickets for air tours and daily Colorado River trips; buy a national-park pass, and access the park by special entry lanes. ⊠*Hwy. 64/U.S. 180, 1 mi south of the south entrance, Box 3309, Tusayan* ☎*928/638–2203 or 928/638–2468* 🖶*928/638–4641* ⊕*www.explorethecanyon.com* 🎫*$12.78 for adults, $9.59 for children (tickets purchased online cost $9.51 for*

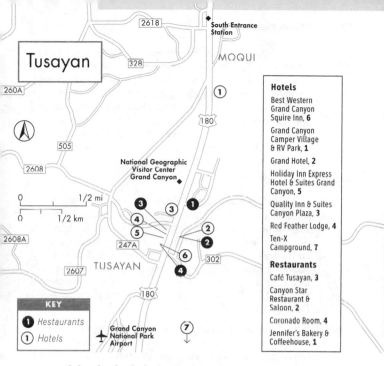

Tusayan

260A

2618

328

South Entrance Station

MOQUI

260A

①

180

505

2608

National Geographic
Visitor Center
Grand Canyon

| 0 | 1/2 mi |
| 0 | 1/2 km |

2608A

❸ ❸ ❶

④

⑤

247A

❷

❷

⑥

TUSAYAN

2607

❹

302

180

KEY

❶ *Restaurants*

① *Hotels*

Grand Canyon
National Park
Airport

⑦

Hotels

Best Western
Grand Canyon
Squire Inn, **6**

Grand Canyon
Camper Village
& RV Park, **1**

Grand Hotel, **2**

Holiday Inn Express
Hotel & Suites Grand
Canyon, **5**

Quality Inn & Suites
Canyon Plaza, **3**

Red Feather Lodge, **4**

Ten-X
Campground, **7**

Restaurants

Café Tusayan, **3**

Canyon Star
Restaurant &
Saloon, **2**

Coronado Room, **4**

Jennifer's Bakery &
Coffeehouse, **1**

adults, $7 for kids) ⊗*Mar.–Oct., daily 8:30–8:30; Nov.–Feb., daily 10:30–6:30; shows every hr on the ½ hr.*

SPORTS & ACTIVITIES

SIGHTSEEING TOURS

Take a naturalist-guided hike, photography workshop, or driving excursion with National Geographic Expeditions.

National Geographic Visitor Center Grand Canyon. For a different point of view, take a one of the tours offered by the naturalist guides at this popular visitor center. "The Best of the Canyon" tour explores the history and geology on an interpretive walking/driving excursion; "Deep in the Canyon" delves into the depths of the canyon on a day hike; and "Images of the Canyon" focuses on capturing the Grand Canyon's glory on film. ⊠*Hwy. 64/U.S.180, Tusayan* ☎*888/355–0550* ⊕*www.explorethecanyon.com* ⊡*$80–$95* ☐*AE, MC, V* ⊗*Reservations essential.*

BICYCLING

Pedal the depths of the Kaibab National Forest on the **Tusayan Bike Trail** (⊠*Tusayan Ranger District, Tusayan*

☎928/638–2443). Following linked-loop trails at an elevation of 6,750 feet, you can bike as few as 3 mi or as many as 32-mi round-trip along old logging roads through a ponderosa-pine forest. Keep an eye out for elk, mule deer, hawks, eagles, pronghorn antelope, turkeys, coyote, and porcupines. Open for biking year-round (but most feasible from March through October), the trail is accessed on the west side of Highway 64, ½ mi north of Tusayan.

WHERE TO EAT

$$–$$$ ✕**Canyon Star Restaurant & Saloon.** Relax in the rustic dining ☺ room at the Grand Hotel for breakfast, lunch, or dinner. ★ The dinner menu includes steak, fried chicken, barbecue ribs, enchiladas, and salmon. Every evening there's entertainment: live music, karaoke, or Native American dance performances—all great for families. There's even a kids' menu. In the summer, be sure to reserve a table. ✉*Hwy. 64/U.S. 180, Box 3319, Tusayan* ☎928/638–3333 ▤*AE, DC, MC, V.*

$$–$$$ ✕**The Coronado Room.** When pizza and burgers just won't do, the restaurant at the Best Western Grand Canyon Squire Inn is the best upscale choice in Tusayan. The menu encompasses everything from escargot to elk steak. Even though the Coronado Room takes pride in its fine-dining atmosphere, dress is casual and comfortable. Reservations are a good idea, particularly in the busy season. ✉*100 Hwy. 64, Box 130, Grand Canyon* ☎928/638–2681 ▤*AE, D, DC, MC, V* ⊙*No lunch.*

¢–$$ ✕**Café Tusayan.** Homemade pies and local microbrews from Sedona, Flagstaff, and Tucson brighten the menu of standard fare—omelets, salads, burgers, salmon, and prime rib—at this basic restaurant. ✉*Hwy. 64/U.S. 180, Box 1959, Tusayan* ☎928/638–2151 ▤*MC, V.*

¢–$ ✕**Jennifer's Bakery & Coffeehouse.** Stop by this jazzy café for a great cup of coffee and high-speed Wi-Fi access. Open from 7 AM to 10 PM in the summer and 7 AM to 3 PM in the winter, this hip coffeehouse serves up breakfast (omelets, French toast, breakfast burritos, pancakes, and pastries) and lunch (soups, salads, sandwiches, and panini) all day. Cozy couches and a nice selection of games and books add to the relaxing atmosphere. ✉*Hwy. 64/U.S. 180, Tusayan* ☎928/638–3433 ▤*MC, V* ⊙*Dec. and Feb.*

WHERE TO STAY

$$-$$$ ☒ **The Grand Hotel.** At the south end of Tusayan, this popu-
★ lar hotel has bright, clean rooms decorated in Southwestern
colors. The lobby has a stone-and-timber design, cozy seating areas, and Wi-Fi access. Good steaks, Mexican fare, and
barbecue are on the restaurant's menu, and a Starbucks in
the lobby is a bonus. At the bar, you can sit on a saddle that
was once used for canyon mule trips. Native American dancing and cowboy singers lead the live entertainment in the
Canyon Star Wild West Saloon during evenings in the peak
season. **Pros:** Coffee stand for a quick morning pick-me-up;
gift shop stocked with outdoor gear and regional books; satellite TV. **Cons:** No in-room Internet access; restaurant and
lounge hours are not reliable; facilities often closed during
off-season. ⊠*Hwy. 64/U.S. 180, Box 3319, Grand Canyon
86023* ☎*928/638–3333 or 888/634–7263* ☐*928/638–3131*
⊕*www.grandcanyongrandhotel.com* ⊲*119 rooms, 2 suites
*☐*In-hotel: restaurant, bar, public Wi-Fi, pool, gym, laundry
facilities, some pets allowed (fee), no-smoking rooms* ⊟*AE,
D, DC, MC, V.*

$$-$$$ ☒ **Holiday Inn Express Hotel and Suites Grand Canyon.** Clean
and contemporary, this popular hotel offers friendly service
and comfortable rooms, decorated with Southwestern patterns in forest greens, coppery browns, and dark plums.
Vivid watercolors set off the colorful scheme. Before taking
off in the morning, stop at the breakfast room for a relaxed
self-service complimentary meal (served daily from 6.30 AM
to 9:30 AM). Selections include everything from fresh fruit
and pastries to biscuits and gravy and hard-boiled eggs.
Pros: Rooms are clean and updated from 2006 renovations; fabulous complimentary breakfast; high-speed Internet access. **Cons:** Plain rooms; unassuming exterior. ⊠*Hwy.
64/U.S. 180, Box 3245, Grand Canyon 86023* ☎*928/638–
3000 or 888/473–2269* ☐*928/638–0123* ⊕*www.grand
canyon.hiexpress.com* ⊲*164 rooms, 30 suites* ☐*In-room:
refrigerator (some), Ethernet. In-hotel: pool* ⊟*AE, D, DC,
MC, V* ⊚*BP.*

$$-$$$ ☒ **Quality Inn & Suites Canyon Plaza.** The outdoor pool is a
hit here in the summer. In the winter, head to the tropical
atrium for a long soak in the indoor hot tub. Decorated
in subtle Southwestern shades, the rooms offer clean com-
fort and several amenities (some rooms have balconies and
refrigerators). The family-friendly restaurant offers three
buffets as well as a full menu serving up salads, burgers,

6

prime rib, and seafood. **Pros:** High-speed Internet; complimentary continental breakfast; waterfall-fed hot tub is a hit with travel-weary guests. **Cons:** Unattractive setting located behind the IMAX theater; busy parking lot; popular lodging for tour groups. ⊠*Hwy. 64/U.S. 180, Box 520, Grand Canyon 86023* ☎*928/638–2673 or 800/995–2521* 🖷*928/638–9537* ⊕*www.grandcanyonqualityinn.com* ➥*176 rooms, 56 suites* ♿*In-room: refrigerator (some), Wi-Fi. In-hotel: restaurant, bar, pool* ⊟*AE, D, DC, MC, V* |○|*CP.*

$–$$$ ⌘**Best Western Grand Canyon Squire Inn.** About 1 mi south
☾ of the park's south entrance, this motel lacks the historic
★ charm of the older lodges at the canyon rim, but has more amenities, including a small cowboy museum in the lobby, a salon, and an upscale gift shop. Children enjoy the bowling alley, arcade, and outdoor swimming pool. Rooms are spacious and furnished in Southwestern style. Those in the rear have a view of the woods. The Coronado Dining Room has an adventurous menu and good service. Wireless Internet service is available in the lobby, and all rooms have broadband. There also are billiards, bowling, and a video-game room. **Pros:** A cool pool in the summer and steamy sauna for cold winter nights; children's activities at the Family Fun Center; high-speed Internet. **Cons:** Lackluster, characterless rooms; hall noise can be an issue with all of the in-hotel activities. ⊠*100 Hwy. 64, Box 130, Grand Canyon 86023* ☎*928/638–2681 or 800/622–6966* 🖷*928/638–2782* ⊕*www.grandcanyonsquire.com* ➥*250 rooms, 4 suites* ♿*In-room: refrigerator (some), Ethernet. In-hotel: restaurant, pool, gym, concierge, no-smoking rooms* ⊟*AE, D, DC, MC, V.*

$$ ⌘**Red Feather Lodge.** This motel and adjacent hotel are a good value, with an outdoor pool and seasonal hot tub. A Southwestern theme dominates the large rooms. The lodge's Café Tusayan serves standard American food. The motel portion of the lodge is closed January through March, except to guests with pets and smokers. The rooms have cable TV with movies and video games, and there is Internet access in the rooms and lobby, though there is a fee to use the service. **Pros:** Elevator access; good availability; complimentary continental breakfast. **Cons:** This older hotel shows more wear and tear than other nearby lodging facilities; fee charged for Internet access. ⊠*Hwy. 64/U.S. 180, Box 1460, Grand Canyon 86023* ☎*928/638–2414 or 800/538–2345* 🖷*928/638–9216* ⊕*www.redfeatherlodge.*

com ☎212 rooms, 1 suite ⌂In-room: Wi-Fi, In-hotel: restaurant, pool, gym, some pets allowed (fee), no-smoking rooms ▤AE, D, DC, MC, V ⦿CP.

WHERE TO CAMP

$$–$$$ ⛺**Grand Canyon Camper Village and RV Park.** More of a city than a village, this popular RV park and campground has 200 utility hookups and 50 tent sites. Reservations are a good idea during the busy spring and summer seasons. ✉Off Hwy. 64/U.S. 180, Grand Canyon ⌖Box 490, Grand Canyon 86023 ☎928/638–2887 ☞200 full hookups, 50 tent sites ⌂Flush toilets, full hookups, dump station, drinking water, showers, picnic tables, general store, play area ⊙Mar.–Nov.

$ ⛺**Ten-X Campground.** Two miles south of Tusayan, this campground offers 70 sites with water and pit toilets but no electrical hookups or showers. Campsites are first-come, first-served, except for the two group sites—one accommodates 100 campers and the other 50—which require reservations. Unlike the campgrounds in the park itself, campfires are allowed. Learn about the surrounding ponderosa-pine forest on a self-guided nature trail or check out one of the evening ranger-led weekend programs. ✉Kaibab National Forest, 9 mi south of the park, east of Hwy. 64/U.S. 180 ⌖Tusayan Ranger District, Box 3088, Grand Canyon 86023 ☎928/638–2443 ⊕www.fs.fed.us/r3/kai ☞70 tent sites, 2 group sites ⌂Grills, vault toilets, drinking water, fire pits, picnic tables ⌖Reservations required for group sites only ⊙Open May–Sept.

WILLIAMS

35 mi west of Flagstaff on I– 40 and AZ 64. 59 mi south of Grand Canyon Village.

At the turn of the 20th century, Williams was a rough-and-tumble town replete with saloons and bordellos. Today, it reflects a much milder side of the Wild West, with 3,190 residents and some 2,500 motel rooms. Wander along main street, named—like the town—after mountain man Bill Williams, and indulge in Route 66 nostalgia. There are antiques shops, cozy eateries, and the ever-present souvenir and T-shirt stores.

The town sits at 6,700 feet in the world's largest stand of ponderosa pines. Often considered just a jumping-off point for the Grand Canyon (it's only an hour away from the South Rim by car and a little more than two hours by train), Williams is temperate in summer, offers skiing in the winter, and is within minutes of seven mountain lakes.

☺ Children enjoy the **Grand Canyon Deer Farm**, a petting zoo with pygmy goats and deer, including fawns born every June, July, and August. Buffalo, pot-bellied pigs, marmosets, reindeer, and exotic birds are also in residence. ⊠6769 *E. Deer Farm Rd., 8 mi east of Williams off I-40, Exit 171* ☎*928/635-4073 or 800/926-3337* ⊕*www.deerfarm.com* ⊠*Adults $7.* ⊙*Jan.–mid-Mar. and mid-Oct.–Dec., daily 10–5; mid-Mar.–mid-Oct., daily 9–6, weather permitting.*

☺ In 1989 service on the **Grand Canyon Railway** was reinaugurated along a route first established in 1901. The 65-mi trek from Williams Depot to the South Rim (2¼ hours each way) takes the vintage train through prairie, ranch, and national-park land to the log-cabin train depot in Grand Canyon Village. You won't see the Grand Canyon from the train, but you can walk or catch the shuttle at the Grand Canyon Railway Station. The ride includes refreshments, commentary, and corny but fun onboard entertainment by Wild West characters from the Cataract Creek Gang. Some passengers ride in restored 1923 cars. Club Class, with its fully stocked mahogany bar and complimentary morning pastries and coffee, costs an additional $20. A First-Class ($60 upgrade), Deluxe Observation Dome, or Luxury Parlor Car ($85 to $95 upgrade) ticket gets you continental breakfast and complimentary afternoon champagne and snacks. Both Coach and Club Classes provide the basics, with padded benches to sit on and ceiling fans to keep you cool; the other three classes provide much more comfortable seating and air-conditioning. Your pet can stay at the Pet Resort while you ride the train.

Even if you don't take the train, it's worth visiting the **Williams Depot,** where the trains depart. It was built in 1908 to replace the terminal where the Williams Visitor Center now resides. Attractions at the depot include a passenger car and the locomotive of a turn-of-the-20th-century steam train, two gift shops where you can find bizarre souvenirs such as a tie that plays "I've Been Working on the Railroad," and Max and Thelma's a full-service restaurant. ⊠*Williams Depot, 233 N. Grand Canyon Blvd. at Fray*

Marcos Blvd. ☎*800/843–8724 railway reservations and information* ⊕*www.thetrain.com* 🎫*$60–$170 round-trip and $8 national park entrance fee* ⊙*Departs daily from Williams in the morning, from South Rim in the afternoon (actual times vary throughout the year).*

☾ **Planes of Fame Museum.** At the junction of U.S. Highway 180 and State Route 64 in Valle, 30 mi north of Williams, this satellite of the Air Museum Planes of Fame in Chino, California, is a good stop for those interested in airplanes. It chronicles the history of aviation with an array of historic and modern aircraft. One of the featured pieces is a C-121A Constellation "Bataan," the personal aircraft of General MacArthur used during the Korean War. Since the planes are in flying condition, visitors are not allowed inside the cockpits. ✉*755 Mustang Way, Valle* ☎*928/635–1000* ⊕*www.planesoffame.org* 🎫*$5.95* ⊙*Daily 9–5.*

The **Williams/Forest Service Visitors Center,** also housing the Williams–Grand Canyon Chamber of Commerce and National Forest Service office, is the former passenger-train depot, built in 1901. Its brick walls still show graffiti scrawled by early railroad workers and hobos. A small bookstore offers a selection of regional materials and an interactive exhibit on the history of the town and Route 66. ✉*200 W. Railroad Ave., at Grand Canyon Blvd.* ☎*928/635–1418 or 800/863–0546* ⊕*www.williamscham ber.com* ⊙*daily 8–5 Sept–May; June–Aug., daily 8–6:30.*

SPORTS & THE OUTDOORS

BICYCLING

Cyclists can enjoy the scenery along the abandoned sections of Route 66 on the Historic Route 66 Mountain Bike Tour. Maps of the tour, which include the 6-mi Ash Fork Hill Trail and the 5-mi Devil Dog Trail, are available at the Williams Visitor Center.

FISHING

Fish for trout, crappie, catfish, and smallmouth bass at a number of lakes surrounding Williams. Anglers age 14 and older are required to obtain a fishing license from the **Arizona Game and Fish Department** (⌂*3500 S. Lake Mary Rd., Flagstaff 86001* ☎*928/774–5045* ⊕*www.gf.state.az.us*) to fish on public land.

SKIING

ⓒ **Elk Ridge Ski and Outdoor Recreation** (✉*875 Ski Run Rd.* ⬧*7596 Buckridge Dr., 86046* ☎*928/814–5038* ⊕*www. elkridgeski.com*) is usually open from mid-December through much of March for skiing, weather permitting; however, the resort is actually open year-round, though only the carpet-tubing flumes and restaurants are open when there's no snow. There are four groomed runs (including one for beginners), areas suitable for cross-country skiing, and a hill set aside for tubing during ski season. The lodge rents skis, snowboards, and inner tubes. From Williams, take South 4th Street for 2 mi, and then turn right at the sign and go another 1½ mi.

WHERE TO EAT

$-$$ ✕**Pancho McGillicuddy's.** Established in 1893 as the Cabinet
★ Saloon, this restaurant is on the National Register of Historic Places. Gone are the spittoons and pipes—the dining area now has Mexican-inspired decor and such specialties as "armadillo eggs," the local name for deep-fried jalapeños stuffed with cheese. Other favorites are the fish tacos, buzzard wings—better known as hot wings—and the pollo verde (chicken breasts smothered in a sauce of cheese, sour cream, and green chiles). The bar—on the smoking side of the restaurant—has TVs tuned to sporting events and pours more than 30 tequilas. ✉*141 Railroad Ave.* ☎*928/635–4150* ⊟*AE, D, MC, V.*

$-$$ ✕**Rod's Steak House.** You can't miss this steak house with the fiberglass Hereford cow out front. The emphasis here is on meat—sizzling mesquite-broiled steaks, prime rib, and the like. The local favorite is Rod's special steak, a hefty sirloin dipped in sugar and grilled over mesquite. Other specialties include chicken, ribs, and seafood. ✉*301 E. Rte. 66* ☎*928/635–2671* ⊟*D, MC, V* ⊘*Closed Sun.*

★ **Fodor's**Choice ✕**Cruisers Café 66.** Talk about nostalgia. Imag-
¢-$$ ine your favorite 1950s-style, high-school hangout—with cocktail service. Good burgers, salads, and malts are family-priced, but a choice steak is available, too, for $25. The large mural of the town's heydey along the "Mother Road" and historic cars out front make this a Route 66 favorite. Kids especially enjoy the relaxed atmosphere. ✉*233 W. Rte. 66* ☎*928/635–2445* ⊟*AE, DC, MC, V.*

¢–$ ✕**Pine Country Restaurant.** This spotless restaurant is across from the Grand Canyon Railway Depot. Owner Dee Seehorn serves homemade pies and hearty meals such as country-fried steak and hamburgers. The crafts that make most of the decor are handmade by local artists and for sale. Open daily at 5:30 AM, the restaurant serves breakfast, lunch, and dinner; for an extra 15%, they will deliver to any hotel in town. ✉*107 N. Grand Canyon Blvd.* ☎*928/635–9718* ▭*AE, D, MC, V.*

¢ ✕**Grand Canyon Coffee & Café.** You'll find good espresso drinks here, along with wonderful hot sandwiches. The mountain-man sandwich is piled-high roast beef with cheddar cheese and onions on sourdough, or try the English-style fish-and-chips. ✉*125 W. Rte. 66* ☎*928/635–4907* ▭*AE, MC, V*

¢ ✕**Twisters.** Get your kicks on Route 66 at this old-fashioned soda fountain and gift shop. Dine on hamburgers and hot dogs, or get a famous Twisters sundae, a Route 66 Beer Float, or a cherry phosphate—all to the sounds of hip-shaking 1950s tunes. The adjoining gift shop is a blast from the past with Route 66 merchandise, classic Coca-Cola memorabilia, and fanciful items celebrating the careers of such characters as Betty Boop, James Dean, Elvis, and Marilyn Monroe. ✉*417 E. Rte. 66* ☎*928/635–0266* ⊕*www. route66place.com* ▭*AE, D, MC, V.*

WHERE TO STAY

$$–$$$ ▣**Sheridan House Inn.** Nestled among 2 acres of pine trees
★ near Route 66, this B&B has outside decks looking to the tall ponderosa pines and a flagstone patio with a hot tub. Most of the average-sized bedrooms have king beds and marble bathrooms. The game room has puzzles, board games, and VCRs, and the entertainment room has a pool table and piano. Hearty breakfasts that include scrambled eggs, fruit plates, bacon, sausage, and breakfast potatoes plus a specialty item such as eggs Benedict or buttermilk pancakes will ready you for the hour-long drive to the canyon. K.C. and Mary Seidner are gracious hosts who will gladly help guests plan itineraries. ✉*460 E. Sheridan Ave., 86046* ☎*928/635–9441 or 888/635–9345* ⊕*www. grandcanyonbedandbreakfast.com* ⊷*6 rooms, 2 suites* ⌂*In-room: no a/c, VCR, Wi-Fi. In-hotel: restaurant, no elevator* ▭*AE, D, MC, V* ⦿*BP.*

$-$$$ ⊞ **Grand Canyon Railway Hotel.** This hotel was designed to
★ resemble the train depot's original Fray Marcos lodge. Neo-
classical Greek columns flank the grand entrance leading
into a lobby with maplewood balustrades, an enormous
flagstone fireplace, and oil paintings of the Grand Canyon
by local artist Kenneth McKenna. The pleasant Southwest-
ern-style accommodations have large bathrooms. Adjacent
to the lobby is Spenser's, a pub with an ornate 19th-century
hand-carved bar. ⊠*235 N. Grand Canyon Blvd., 86046*
☏*928/635–4010 or 800/843–8724* ⊕*www.thetrain.com*
⌂*287 rooms, 10 suites* ⚴*In-hotel: bar, pool, gym, no-
smoking rooms* ⊟*AE, D, MC, V.*

$-$$ ⊞ **Mountainside Inn Resort & Convention Center.** At the east
entrance to town, this basic motel has comfortable rooms,
a good American restaurant called Miss Kitty's Steakhouse,
and country-and-western bands in summer. ⊠*642 E. Rte.
66, 86046* ☏*928/635–4431 or 800/462–9381* ⚏*928/635–
2292* ⌂*95 rooms, 1 suite* ⚴*In-hotel: restaurant, pool, no
elevator* ⊟*AE, D, MC, V.*

$-$$ ⊞ **The Red Garter Bed and Breakfast Inn.** This restored 1897
saloon and bordello is now a small, antique-filled B&B.
Guest rooms are on the 2nd floor; the Best Gal's room has
its own sitting room overlooking the train station. All four
rooms (two are interior, with skylights but no windows) are
fairly quiet, but some trains use the spur tracks in the off-
hours. Even if you don't stay here, the fresh pastries served
in the 1st-floor coffee shop are worth a stop. ⊠*137 W.
Railroad Ave., 86046* ☏*928/635–1484 or 800/328–1484*
⊕*www.redgarter.com* ⌂*4 rooms* ⚴*In-room: dial-up, Wi-
Fi. In-hotel: restaurant, public Wi-Fi, no kids under 8, no-
smoking rooms, no elevator* ⊟*D, MC, V* ⏃*CP* ⊘*Closed
Dec.–mid-Feb.*

$ ⊞ **The Canyon Motel & RV Park.** Rail cars, cabooses, and cot-
⟳ tages make up this 13-acre property on the outskirts of
Williams. The two best rooms are in the 1929 Santa Fe red
cabooses: they are family-friendly, with two sides separated
by a bathroom, giving parents a little privacy. The original wooden floor and tool equipment add to the authen-
ticity in one caboose. The other caboose looks much like
an old Wild West train car inside. The flagstone cottage
rooms built from the local sandstone known for its varie-
gated colors look much like standard hotel rooms. A Pull-
man passenger car holds three rooms (rail-car suites), each
with its own bathroom. The motel also has a few dry (no

water available) campsites and a 47-space RV park with full hookups, opened in 2006. A general store with milk, soda, RV supplies, and a few other basics opened in 2007. ✉*1900 E. Rodeo Rd. Rte. 66, 86046* ☎*928/635–9371 or 800/482–3955* 🖷*928/635–4138* ⊕*www.thecanyon motel.com* ↩*18 rooms, 5 rail-car suites* ◻*In-room: no a/c (some), no phone, refrigerator, VCR (some). In-hotel: pool, public Wi-Fi, no elevator* ▭*D, MC, V* ⧫*CP.*

WHERE TO CAMP

Both developed and undeveloped campsites are available on a first-come, first-served basis in the **Kaibab National Forest** (☎*928/635–4061 or 800/863–0546* ⊕*www.fs.fed. us/r3/kai*), which surrounds Williams and extends to the Grand Canyon encompassing Cataract Lake, Kaibab Lake, Dogtown Lake, and White Horse Lake.

SHOPPING

Whether you're looking for Grand Canyon souvenirs, Western kitsch, or the best in Native American art and jewelry, you'll likely find it in the shops on Historic Route 66. The cheery **Rustic Raspberry** (✉*309 W. Rte. 66* ☎*928/635–3024*) has a homey, spicy smell along with country crafts for sale.

FLAGSTAFF

146 mi northwest of Phoenix, 27 mi north of Sedona via Oak Creek Canyon.

Few travelers slow down long enough to explore Flagstaff, a town of 54,000, known locally as "Flag"; most stop only to spend the night at one of the town's many motels before making the last leg of the trip to the Grand Canyon, 80 mi north. Flag makes a good base for day trips to Native American ruins and the Navajo and Hopi reservations, as well as to the Petrified Forest National Park and the Painted Desert, but the city is a worthwhile destination in its own right. Set against a lovely backdrop of pine forests and the snowcapped San Francisco Peaks, downtown Flagstaff retains a frontier flavor.

In summer, Phoenix residents head here, seeking relief from the desert heat, since at any time of the year temperatures in Flagstaff are about 20°F cooler than in Phoenix. They also come to Flagstaff in winter: to ski at the small Arizona

Snowbowl, about 15 mi northeast of town among the San Francisco Peaks.

EXPLORING FLAGSTAFF

WHAT TO SEE

Arizona Snowbowl. Although still one of Flagstaff's largest attractions, years of drought have made snowy slopes a luxury. Fortunately, visitors can enjoy the beauty of the area year-round. The Agassiz ski lift climbs to a height of 11,500 feet in 25 minutes, and doubles as a sky ride through the Coconino National Forest in summer. From this vantage point, you can see up to 70 mi; views may even include the North Rim of the Grand Canyon. There's a lodge at the base with a restaurant and bar. To reach the ski area, take U.S. 180 north from Flagstaff; it's 7 mi from the Snowbowl exit to the skyride entrance. *⊠Snowbowl Rd., North Flagstaff* ☎928/779–1951 *⊕www.arizonasnow-bowl.com* *⊠Skyride $10* *☉Skyride: Memorial Day–early Sept., daily 10–4; early Sept.–mid-Oct., Fri.–Sun. 10–4, weather permitting.*

Historic Downtown District. Storied Route 66 runs right through the heart of downtown Flagstaff. The late-Victorian, Tudor Revival, and early–art deco architecture in this district recalls the town's heyday as a logging and railroad center. A walking-tour map of the area is available at the visitor center in the Tudor Revival–style **Santa Fe Depot** (*⊠1 E. Rte. 66, Downtown*), an excellent place to begin sightseeing.

Highlights include the 1927 **Hotel Monte Vista** (*⊠100 N. San Francisco St., Downtown⊕www.hotelmontevista. com*), built after a community fund-raiser brought in $200,000 in 60 days. The construction was promoted as a way to bolster the burgeoning tourism in the region, and the hotel was held publicly until the early 1960s. The 1888 **Babbitt Brothers Building** (*⊠12 E. Aspen Ave., Downtown*) was constructed as a building-supply store and then turned into a department store by David Babbitt, the mastermind of the Babbitt empire. The Babbitts are one of Flagstaff's wealthiest founding families. Bruce Babbitt, the most recent member of the family to wield power and influence, was the governor of Arizona from 1978 through 1987 and Secretary of the Interior under President Clinton (1993–2001). Most of the area's first businesses were saloons catering to railroad construction workers, which was the case with the

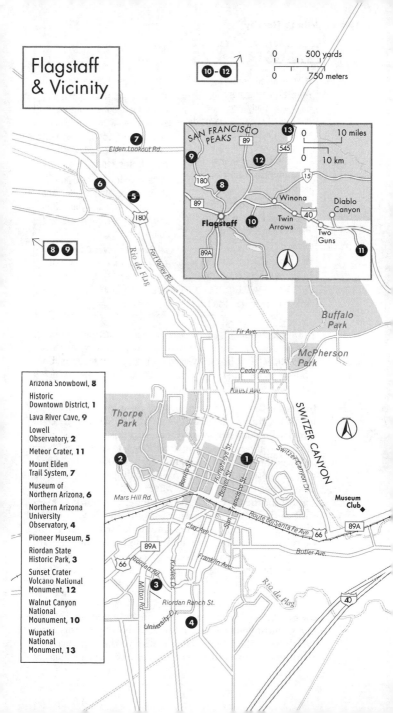

Flagstaff & Vicinity

0 — 500 yards
0 — 750 meters

10 – 12

SAN FRANCISCO PEAKS

0 — 10 miles
0 — 10 km

89
545
180
89A
89
15
Winona
Flagstaff
Twin Arrows
40
Two Guns
Diablo Canyon

Elden Lookout Rd.

Rio de Flag
Fort Valley Rd.

Buffalo Park

McPherson Park

SWITZER CANYON

Fir Ave.
Cedar Ave.
Forest Ave.

Thorpe Park

Switzer Canyon Dr.

Museum Club

Humphreys St.
Beaver St.
San Francisco St.

Mars Hill Rd.

Route 66/Santa Fe Ave.
66
89A

Clay Ave.
Franklin Ave.
Butler Ave.

Riordan Rd.
Knoles Dr.
Milton Rd.

89A
66

Riordan Ranch St.

University Dr.

Rio de Flag
40

Arizona Snowbowl, **8**

Historic Downtown District, **1**

Lava River Cave, **9**

Lowell Observatory, **2**

Meteor Crater, **11**

Mount Elden Trail System, **7**

Museum of Northern Arizona, **6**

Northern Arizona University Observatory, **4**

Pioneer Museum, **5**

Riordan State Historic Park, **3**

Sunset Crater Volcano National Monument, **12**

Walnut Canyon National Monument, **10**

Wupatki National Monument, **13**

FLAGSTAFF TIPS

■ You can see most of Flagstaff's attractions in a day—especially if you visit the Lowell Observatory or the Northern Arizona University Observatory in the evening, which is also when the Museum Club is best experienced.

■ Consult the schedule of tour times if you want to visit the Riordan State Historic Park.

■ Devote at least an hour to the excellent Museum of Northern Arizona.

■ The Historic Railroad District is a good place for lunch.

■ If you're a skier, spend part of a winter's day at Arizona Snowbowl; in summer you can spend a couple of hours on the sky ride and scenic trails at the top.

■ Take your time enjoying the trails on Mount Elden and remember to pace yourself in the higher elevations; allow a full day for hiking.

■ The Lava River Cave is an easy—if dark—hike that can be comfortably done in an hour.

1888 **Vail Building** (⊠*5 N. San Francisco St., Downtown*), a brick art deco–influenced structure covered with stucco in 1939. It now houses Crystal Magic, a New Age shop. ⊠*Downtown Historic District, Rte. 66 north to Birch Ave., and Beaver St. east to Agassiz St.*

Lava River Cave. Subterranean-lava flow formed this mile-long cave roughly 700,000 years ago. Once you descend into its boulder-strewn maw, the cave is spacious, with 40-foot ceilings—but claustrophobes take heed: about halfway through, the cave tapers to a 4-foot-high squeeze that can be a bit unnerving. A 40°F chill pervades the cave throughout the year so take warm clothing. To reach the turnoff for the cave, go approximately 9 mi north of Flagstaff on U.S. 180, then turn west onto FR 245. Turn left at the intersection of FR 171 and look for the sign to the cave. The trip is approximately 45 minutes from Flagstaff. Although the cave is on National Forest Service property, the only thing here is an interpretive sign, so it's definitely something you tackle at your own risk. ■TIP➔**Pack a flashlight (or two).** ⊠*FR 171B.*

☾ ★ **Lowell Observatory.** In 1894, Boston businessman, author, and scientist Percival Lowell founded this observatory from which he studied Mars. His theories of the existence of a ninth planet sowed the seeds for the discovery of Pluto at

Lowell in 1930 by Clyde Tombaugh. The 6,500-square-foot Steele Visitor Center hosts exhibits and lectures and has a gift shop. Several interactive exhibits—among them Pluto Walk, a scaled-down version of the solar system—appeal to children. A new Discovery Channel telescope is anticipated for 2009 and you are invited, on some evenings, to peer through the 24-inch Clark telescope. Day and evening viewings are offered year-round, but call ahead for a schedule. ■TIP→**The observatory dome is open and unheated, so dress for the outdoors.** To reach the observatory, less than 2 mi from downtown, drive west on Route 66, which resumes its former name, Santa Fe Avenue, before it merges into Mars Hill Road. ✉ *1400 W. Mars Hill Rd., West Flagstaff* ☎ *928/774–3358* ⊕ *www.lowell.edu* ✑ *$6* ☉ *Visitor center and night viewing hrs change seasonally; call ahead.*

Mount Elden Trail System. Most trails in the 35-mi-long Mount Elden Trail System lead to views from the dormant volcanic field, across the vast ponderosa-pine forest, all the way to Sedona. The most challenging trail in the Mount Elden system, which happens to be the route with the most rewarding views, is along the steep switchbacks of the **Elden Lookout Trail** (✉ *off U.S. 89, 3 mi east of downtown Flagstaff*). If you traverse the full 3 mi to the top, keep your focus on the landscape rather than the tangle of antennae and satellite dishes that greet you at the top. The 4-mi-long **Sunset Trail** (✉ *off U.S. 180, 3 mi north of downtown Flagstaff, then 6 mi east on FR 420 [Schultz Pass Rd.]*) proceeds with a gradual pitch through the pine forest, emerging onto a narrow ridge nicknamed the Catwalk. By all means take pictures of the stunning valley views, but make sure your feet are well placed. ■TIP→**The access road to this trail is closed in winter.**

☾ ★ **Museum of Northern Arizona.** This institution, founded in 1928, is respected worldwide for its research and its collections centering on the natural and cultural history of the Colorado Plateau. Among the permanent exhibitions are an extensive collection of Navajo rugs and a Hopi kiva (men's ceremonial chamber). A gallery devoted to area geology is usually a hit with children: it includes a life-size model dilophosaurus, a carnivorous dinosaur that once roamed northern Arizona. Outdoors, a life-zone exhibit shows the changing vegetation from the bottom of the Grand Canyon to the highest peak in Flagstaff. A nature trail, open only in summer, heads down across a small stream into a canyon and up into an aspen grove. In summer the museum hosts exhibits and the works of Native American artists, whose wares are also sold in the museum gift shop. ✉*3101 N. Fort Valley Rd., North Flagstaff* ☎*928/774–5213* ⊕*www. musnaz.org* ✉*$5* ⊙*Daily 9–5.*

Northern Arizona University Observatory. The observatory, with its 24-inch telescope, was built in 1952 by Dr. Arthur Adel, a scientist at Lowell Observatory whose study of infrared astronomy pioneered research into molecules that absorb light passing through the Earth's atmosphere. Today's studies of Earth's shrinking ozone layer rely on some of Dr. Adel's early work. Visitors to the observatory—which houses one of the largest telescopes that the public is allowed to move and manipulate—are usually hosted by friendly students and faculty members of the university's Department of Physics and Astronomy. ✉*Bldg. 47, Northern Arizona Campus Observatory, Dept. of Physics and Astronomy, S. San Francisco St., just north of Walkup Skydome, University* ☎*928/523–8121 weekdays, 928/523–7170 Fri. night* ✉*Free* ⊙*Viewings Fri. 7:30–10* PM, *weather permitting.*

Pioneer Museum. The Arizona Historical Society operates this museum in a volcanic-rock building constructed in 1908. The structure was Coconino County's first hospital for the poor, and the current displays include one of the depressingly small nurses' rooms, an old iron lung, and a reconstructed doctor's office. Most of the exhibits, however, touch on more cheerful aspects of Flagstaff history—like road signs and children's toys. The museum holds a folk-crafts festival on July 4, with blacksmiths, weavers, spinners, quilters, and candle makers. Their crafts, and those of other local artisans, are sold in the museum's gift shop. The museum is part of the Fort Valley Park complex, in a wooded residential section at the northwest end of town. ✉*2340 N. Fort Valley Rd., North Flagstaff* ☎*928/774–6272* ✉*$3* ⊙*Mon.–Sat. 9–5.*

Riordan State Historic Park. This must-see artifact of Flagstaff's logging heyday is near Northern Arizona University. The centerpiece is a mansion built in 1904 for Michael and Timothy Riordan, lumber-baron brothers who married two sisters. The 13,300-square-foot, 40-room log-and-stone structure—designed by Charles Whittlesley, who was also responsible for the El Tovar Hotel at the Grand Canyon—contains furniture by Gustav Stickley, father of the American Arts and Crafts design movement. One room holds "Paul Bunyan's shoes," a 2-foot-long pair of boots made by Timothy in his workshop. Everything on display is original to the house. The mansion may be explored on a guided tour only, and reservations are suggested. ⊠ *409 W. Riordan Rd., University* ☎*928/779–4395* ⊕*www.pr.state. az.us* ⊠*$6* ⊙*May–Oct., daily 8:30–5, with tours on the hr 9–4; Nov.–Apr., daily 10:30–5, with tours on the hr 11–4.*

SPORTS & THE OUTDOORS

HIKING & ROCK CLIMBING

You can explore Arizona's alpine tundra in the San Francisco Peaks, part of the Coconino National Forest, where more than 80 species of plants grow on the upper elevations. The habitat is fragile, so hikers are asked to stay on established trails (there are lots of them). The altitude here will make even the hardiest hikers breathe a little harder, so anyone with cardiac or respiratory problems should be cautious about overexertion. ■TIP➔**Flatlanders should give themselves at least a day or two to adjust to the altitude.**

The rangers of the **Coconino National Forest** (⊠*1824 S. Thompson St., North Flagstaff* ☎*928/527–3600* ⊕*www. fs.fed.us/r3/coconino*) maintain many of the region's trails and can provide you with details on hiking in the area; the forest's main office is open weekdays 7:30 to 4:30.

Flagstaff is in the **Peaks District** (⊠*Peaks Ranger Station, 5075 N. U.S. 89, East Flagstaff* ☎*928/526–0866*) of the Coconino National Forest, and there are many trails to explore. The **Humphreys Peak Trail** (⊠*Trailhead: Snowbowl Rd., 7 mi north of U.S. 180*) is 9-mi round-trip, with a vertical climb of 3,843 feet to the summit of Arizona's highest mountain (12,643 feet). Those who don't want a long hike can do just the first mile of the adjacent, 5-mi-long **Kachina Trail** (⊠*Trailhead: Snowbowl Rd., 7 mi north of U.S. 180*); gently rolling, this route is surrounded by huge stands of aspen and offers fantastic vistas. In fall, changing leaves paint the landscape shades of yellow, russet, and amber.

Vertical Relief Rock Gym (⊠*205 S. San Francisco St., Downtown* ☎*928/556–9909*) has the tallest indoor climbing walls in the Southwest as well as climbing excursions throughout the Flagstaff area.

HORSEBACK RIDING

The wranglers at **Hitchin' Post Stables** (⊠*4848 Lake Mary Rd., South Flagstaff* ☎*928/774–1719*) lead rides into Walnut Canyon and operate horseback or horse-drawn wagon rides with sunset barbecues. In winter they'll take you through Coconino National Forest on a sleigh.

MOUNTAIN BIKING

With more than 30 mi of challenging trails a short ride from town, it was inevitable that one of Flagstaff's best-kept secrets would leak out. Mountain biking on Mount Elden is on par with that of more celebrated trails in Colorado and Utah.

The **Coconino National Forest** has some of the best trails in the region. A good place to start is the **Lower Oldham Trail** (⊠*Trailhead: Cedar St.*), which originates on the north end of Buffalo Park in Flagstaff; there's a large meadow with picnic areas and an exercise path. The terrain rolls, climbing about 800 feet in 3 mi, and the trail is technical in spots but easy enough to test your tolerance of the elevation. Many fun trails spur off this one. They're all hemmed in by roads and cabins so it's difficult to get too lost.

The very popular **Schultz Creek Trail** (⊠*Trailhead: Schultz Pass Rd., near intersection with U.S. 180*) is fun and suitable for strong beginners, although seasoned experts will be thrilled as well. Most opt to start at the top of the 600-foot-high hill and swoop down the smooth, twisting path through groves of wildflowers and stands of ponderosa pines and aspens, ending at the trailhead 4 giddy mi later.

The **Sunset Trail** (⊠*Trailhead: Elden Lookout Rd., 7 mi from intersection with Schultz Pass Rd.*), near the summit of Mount Elden, affords amazing views off the ridge rendered barren by a 1977 fire. The trail narrows into the aptly nicknamed Catwalk, with precipitous drops a few feet on either side. ■TIP→**Fear, either from the 9,000-foot elevation or the sheer exposure, is not an option. You need to be an at least moderately experienced mountain biker to attempt this trail.** When combined with Elden Lookout Road and Schultz Creek Trail, the usual loop, the trail totals 15 mi and climbs almost 2,000 feet. You can avoid the slog up Mount Elden by parking one vehicle at the top of Elden Lookout Road, at the trailhead, and a friend's vehicle at the bottom.

You can rent mountain bikes, get good advice, and purchase trail maps at **Absolute Bikes** (⊠*18 N. San Francisco St., Downtown* ☎*928/779–5969*). From mid-June through mid-October, the **Flagstaff Nordic Center** (⊠*U.S. 180, 16*

mi north of Flagstaff, North Flagstaff ☎*928/220–0550*
⊕*www.flagstaffnordiccenter.com*) opens its cross-country
trails to mountain bikers. **Mountain Sports** (⊠*24 N. San
Francisco St., Downtown* ☎*928/226–2885 or 800/286–
5156*) has competitive rates for bike rentals. A map of the
Urban Trails System, available at the Flagstaff Visitor Center
(⊠*1 E. Rte. 66, Downtown* ☎*928/774–9541 or 800/842–
7293*), details biking options in town.

SKIING & SNOWBOARDING

The ski season usually starts in mid-December and ends in
mid-April. The **Arizona Snowbowl** (⊠*Snowbowl Rd., North
Flagstaff* ☎*928/779–1951, 928/779–4577 snow report*
⊕*www.arizonasnowbowl.com*), 7 mi north of Flagstaff off
U.S. 180, has 32 downhill runs (37% beginner, 42% intermediate, and 21% advanced), four chairlifts, and a vertical drop of 2,300 feet. There are a couple of good bump
runs, but it's better for beginners or those with moderate
skill; serious skiers take a road trip to Teluride. Still, it's a
fun place to spend the day. Snowboarders share trails with
downhill skiers. The Hart Prairie Lodge has an equipment-
rental shop and a SKIwee center for ages 4 to 7. All-day
adult lift tickets are $46. Half-day discounts are available,
and group-lesson packages (including two hours of instruc-
tion, an all-day lift ticket, and equipment rental) are a good
buy at $68. A children's program (which includes lunch,
progress card, and full supervision 9–3:30) runs $70. Many
Flagstaff motels offer ski packages, including transportation to Snowbowl.

The **Flagstaff Nordic Center** (⊠*U.S. 180, 16 mi north of
Flagstaff, North Flagstaff* ☎*928/220–0550* ⊕*www.flag-
staffnordiccenter.com*) is 9 mi north of Snowbowl Road.
There are 25 mi of well-groomed cross-country trails here
that are open from 8 to 4 daily, with longer hours on Friday (6 to 9). Coffee, hot chocolate, and snacks are served
at the lodge. You can also rent sleds for a nearby run called
Crowley Pit. A day pass for skiing costs $12 on weekdays
and $15 on weekends. An instruction package costs $40
on weekdays and $45 on weekends, including equipment.
Friday evening trail passes cost $10. To rent equipment by
itself is $15.

WHERE TO EAT

★   ×**Cottage Place.** Regarded by locals as one of the best fine-
$$$–$$$$ dining venues in the area, this restaurant in a cottage built
in 1909 has intimate dining rooms and an extensive wine
list. The menu strays slightly from continental to include
some classic American dishes, such as charbroiled lamb
chops. The grilled herb salmon and the chateaubriand for
two are recommended. Dinner includes soup and salad,
but save room for Chocolate Decadence. ✉*126 W. Cottage
Ave., Downtown* ☎*928/774–8431* ⊕*www.cottageplace.
com* ▤AE, MC, V ⊘*Closed Mon. and Tues. No lunch*

$$–$$$$ ×**Black Bart's Steakhouse Saloon & Old West Theater.** The Wild
West decor at this rollicking, brightly lit barn of a restau-
rant is a bit cornball, but the barbecued chicken is tender
and flavorful; don't expect to see vegetables on your plate
unless they're deep-fried. Northern Arizona University
music students entertain while they wait tables, so don't
be surprised if your server suddenly jumps onstage to belt
out a couple of show tunes. ✉*2760 E. Butler Ave., Downtown* ☎*928/779–3142 or 800/574–4718* ⊕*www.black
bartssteakhouse.com* ▤AE, D, DC, MC, V ⊘*No lunch.*

$$–$$$ ×**Buster's Restaurant.** At lunchtime, families and students
from nearby Northern Arizona University settle into comfy
booths to enjoy fresh seafood, homemade soups, salads,
giant burgers, and steaks. What better environment to
ask Mom or Dad for some extra money, or to discuss that
first semester's report card? Try the *lahvosh* appetizer—a
huge cracker heaped with toppings ranging from smoked
salmon to mushrooms—or the Caesar salad with grilled
Cajun chicken. At night, single professionals and skiers
crowd the bar and work through its impressive beer selection. ✉*1800 S. Milton Rd., University* ☎*928/774–5155*
▤AE, D, DC, MC, V.

$$–$$$ ×**Pasto.** This downtown Italian restaurant—two intimate
dining rooms in adjacent historic buildings—is popular for
good food at reasonable prices. Southern Italian standards
like lasagna and spaghetti with meatballs are on the menu
along with more innovative fare, such as artichoke orzo.
A courtyard in the back, tucked among higher buildings,
has a romantic urban feel. ✉*19 E. Aspen St., Downtown*
☎*928/779–1937* ⊕*www.pastorestaurant.com* ▤D, MC, V
⊘*Closed Tues.*

$–$$ ✕Beaver Street Brewery and Whistle Stop Cafe. Popular among the wood-fired pizzas is the Enchanted Forest, with Brie, portobello mushrooms, roasted red peppers, spinach, and artichoke pesto. Whichever pie you order, expect serious amounts of garlic. Sandwiches, such as the Southwestern chicken with three types of cheese, come with a hefty portion of tasty fries. You won't regret ordering one of the down-home desserts, like the super-gooey chocolate bread pudding. Among the excellent microbrews usually on tap, the raspberry ale is a local favorite. ✉ *11 S. Beaver St., Downtown* ☎ *928/779–0079* ⊕ *www.beaverstreetbrewery. com* ⊟ AE, D, DC, MC, V

¢–$$ ✕Salsa Brava. This cheerful Mexican restaurant, with light-wood booths and colorful designs, eschews heavy Sonoran-style fare in favor of the grilled dishes found in Guadalajara. It's considered the best Mexican food in town—but there's not much competition. The fish tacos are particularly good. On weekends come for a huevos rancheros breakfast. ✉ *2220 E. Rte. 66, East* ☎ *928/779–5293* ⊕ *www. salsabravaflagstaff.com* ⊟ AE, D, MC, V.

¢–$ ✕Bun Huggers. Since 1979, the best burger in town is flipped over a mesquite-fired grill. Also try the tasty, if decadent, deep-fried zucchini served with shredded cheddar cheese and ranch dressing. There's a small salad bar here, but it seems like an afterthought, existing only to heal guilty consciences. ✉ *901 S. Milton Rd., University* ☎ *928/779–3743* ⊟ AE, D, MC, V.

¢–$ ✕Café Espress. The menu is largely vegetarian at this natural-foods restaurant. Stir-fried vegetables, pasta, Mediterranean salads, tempeh burgers, pita pizzas, fish or chicken specials, and wonderful baked goods made on the premises all come at prices that will make you feel good, too. This is a hip place (the work of local artists hangs on the walls) but friendly, and it opens for breakfast every day at 7. ✉ *16 N. San Francisco St., Downtown* ☎ *928/774–0541* ⊟ AE, MC, V.

★ ¢ ✕La Bellavia. At this favorite bohemian breakfast and lunch nook, the trout and eggs platter is the standard—two eggs served with Idaho trout flavored with a hint of lemon, rounded off by a buttermilk pancake. Other options include Swedish oat pancakes, seven-grain French toast, and nine varieties of eggs Benedict. A palette of creative sandwiches and familiar salads makes this a worthwhile lunch stop as well. The café doubles as a gallery for local

6

artists whose work hangs on the walls. If you like your pancakes, you can buy a package of the mix to take home. ⊠*18 S. Beaver St., Downtown* ☎*928/774–8301* ⊟MC, V ⊗*No dinner.*

WHERE TO STAY

★ **⊡Inn at 410.** An inviting alternative to the chain motels
$$–$$$ in Flagstaff, this B&B has a convenient but quiet downtown location. All the accommodations in the beautifully restored 1907 residence are suites with private baths. Monet's Garden is a lovely Jacuzzi suite with fireplace. Pancakes with blue cornmeal and piñon nuts, and curried cornbread pudding with pumpkin sauce highlight a tantalizing breakfast menu. No kids allowed in some rooms. ⊠*410 N. Leroux St., Downtown, 86001* ☎*928/774–0088 or 800/774–2008*🖷*928/774–6354* ⊕*www.inn410.com* ⇨*9 suites* ⚿*In-room: no phone, refrigerator, VCR/DVD. In-hotel: no-smoking rooms, no elevator*⊟MC, V �101*BP.*

★ $$ **⊡Little America of Flagstaff.** The biggest hotel in town is deservedly popular. It's far from the roar of the trains, the grounds are surrounded by evergreen forests, and it's one of the few places in Flagstaff with room service. Plush rooms have comfortable sitting areas with French provincial–style furniture. Other pluses are courtesy van service to the airport and the Amtrak station, and a gift shop with great Southwestern stuff. Don't miss the famous Sunday Brunch with breakfast fare alongside prime rib, seafood, and European-style pastries. ⊠*2515 E. Butler Ave., Downtown, 86004* ☎*928/779–2741 or 800/352–4386* 🖷*928/779–7983* ⊕*www.flagstaff.littleamerica.com* ⇨*248 rooms* ⚿*In-room: kitchen, refrigerator, safe. In-hotel: restaurant, room service, bar, pool, gym, laundry facilities, laundry service, public Wi-Fi, no elevator* ⊟AE, D, DC, MC, V.

$$ **⊡Sled Dog Inn.** This inn is on 4 acres, but its grounds seem vastly larger, since the land borders the immense Coconino National Forest. A big draw here, as the name implies, are the owners' Siberian huskies, which are lovingly cared for. Rooms are contemporary rustic. ⊠*10155 Mountainaire Rd., South Flagstaff, 86001* ☎*928/525–6212 or 800/754–0064* ⊕*www.sleddoginn.com* ⇨*8 rooms, 2 suites* ⚿*In-room: no TV. In-hotel: no kids under 10, no-smoking rooms, no elevator, public Wi-Fi* ⊟AE, D, MC, V 101*CP.*

$$ **Starlight Pines Bed and Breakfast.** If you prefer the clean lines of 1920s design to Victorian froufrou, consider staying at this stylish B&B. Rooms in this residence on the city's east side are lovely, with art deco pieces including Tiffany lamps and other antiques; one room has a private porch, another a fireplace. ✉*3380 E. Lockett Rd., East Flagstaff 86004* ☎*928/527–1912 or 800/752–1912* ⊕*www.starlightpinesbb.com* ⇆*4 rooms* ⌂*In-room: no TV. In-hotel: no-smoking rooms, no elevator, public Wi-Fi*❑D, MC, V ⧉*BP.*

$-$$ **Hotel Monte Vista.** Over the years many Hollywood stars, including Bob Hope and Spencer Tracy, have stayed at this downtown hotel, which is celebrating its 80th anniversary in 2008. It's a quirky, fun place, but renovations have not yet restored it to its heyday. Funky room designs might have golden cherubs descending from an azure ceiling— in the Air Supply Room—or are inspired by the famous guests: framed antique postcards of Western novel book covers hang in the Zane Grey Room. Enjoy live music every Friday and Saturday night. ✉*100 N. San Francisco St., Downtown, 86001* ☎*928/779–6971 or 800/545–3068* 🖷*928/779–2904* ⊕*www.hotelmontevista.com* ⇆*48 rooms* ⌂*In-hotel: restaurant, bars, laundry service, some pets allowed*❑AE, D, MC, V.

¢ **Hotel Weatherford.** With a columned veranda, this hotel, built in 1897, is a dramatic presence at the hub of town. Imbued with a creaky charm, the rooms are spartan and a bit worn around the edges but comfortable. Forgo TV and a telephone for a taste of the Old West. The Exchange Pub downstairs has a bustling nightlife scene. ✉*23 N. Leroux St., Downtown, 86001* ☎*928/779–1919* 🖷*928/773–8951* ⊕*www.weatherfordhotel.com* ⇆*10 rooms, 7 with bath* ⌂*In-room: no a/c, no phone, no TV. In-hotel: restaurant, bars, no elevator*❑AE, D, DC, MC, V.

NIGHTLIFE & THE ARTS

Flagstaff's large college contingent has plenty of places to gather after dark; most are in historic downtown and most charge little or no cover. It's easy to walk from one rowdy spot to the next. For information on what's going on, pick up the free *Flagstaff Live*.

The **Hotel Weatherford** (✉*23 N. Leroux St., Downtown* ☎*928/779–1919*) has a double bill: Charly's hosts late-

6

night jazz and blues bands; the Exchange Pub tends to attract folksy ensembles. The **Mogollon Brewing Company** (✉*15 N. Agassiz St., Downtown* ☎*928/773–8950*) rolls out live music and hardy stout. The **Monte Vista Lounge** (✉*100 N. San Francisco St., Downtown* ☎*928/774–2403*) packs 'em in with nightly live blues, jazz, classic rock, and punk. **San Felipe's Coastal Cantina** (✉*103 N. Leroux, Downtown* ☎*928/779–6000*) is the place for tequila, fish tacos, dancing, and a raucous spring-break atmosphere.

There is no shortage of cultural entertainment in Flagstaff, including several summer festivals.

Flagstaff Cultural Partners/Coconino Center for the Arts (✉*2300 N. Fort Valley Rd., North Flagstaff* ☎*928/779–2300* ⊕*www.culturalpartners.org*) has gallery space for exhibitions, a theater, and performance space. The **Flagstaff Symphony Orchestra** (☎*928/774–5107* ⊕*www.flagstaffsymphony.org*) has year-round musical events. The 1917 **Orpheum Theater** (✉*15 W. Aspen St., Downtown*☎*928/556–1580* ⊕*www.orpheumpresents.com*) features music acts, films, lectures, and plays. **Theatrikos Theatre Company** (✉*11 W. Cherry Ave., Downtown* ☎*928/774–1662* ⊕*www.theatrikos.com*) is a highly regarded performance-art group.

A Celebration of Native American Art (✉*3101 N. Fort Valley Rd., North Flagstaff* ☎*928/774–5211*), featuring exhibits of work by Zuni, Hopi, and Navajo artists, is held at the Museum of Northern Arizona from late May through September.

The **Festival of Science** (☎*800/842–7293* ⊕*www.scifest.org*), in September, is made stellar by Flagstaff's observatories.

SHOPPING

For fine arts and crafts—everything from ceramics and stained glass to weaving and painting—visit the **Artists Gallery** (✉*17 N. San Francisco St., Downtown* ☎*928/773–0958*), a local artists' cooperative. **Babbitt's Backcountry Outfitters** (✉*12 E. Aspen Ave., Downtown* ☎*928/774–4775*) is the place to pick up any sporting goods needs. The **Black Hound Gallerie** (✉*120 N. Leroux St., Downtown*☎*928/774–2323*) specializes in posters, prints, and funky kitsch of all kinds. **Bookman's** (✉*1520 S. Riordan Ranch Rd., University*☎*928/774–0005*) is packed solid with used books on every topic; a cybercafé and live folk music occupy a corner of the store. **Carriage House**

Antique & Gift Mall (✉413 N. San Francisco St., Downtown☎928/774–1337) has 20-odd vendors selling vintage clothing and jewelry, furniture, fine china, and other collectibles. The **Museum of Northern Arizona Gift Shop** (✉3101 N. Fort Valley Rd., University☎928/774–5213) carries high-quality jewelry and crafts. **Winter Sun Trading Company** (✉107 N. San Francisco St., Downtown☎928/774–2884) sells medicinal herbs, jewelry, and crafts. **Zani** (✉9 N. Leroux St., Downtown ☎928/774–9409) stocks hip home furnishings and greeting cards in addition to futons.

SIDE TRIPS NEAR FLAGSTAFF

Travelers heading straight through town bound for the Grand Canyon often neglect the area north and east of Flagstaff but a detour has its rewards. If you don't have time to do everything, take a quick drive to Walnut Canyon—it's only about 15 minutes out of town.

EAST OF FLAGSTAFF

★ **Walnut Canyon National Monument** consists of a group of cliff dwellings constructed by the Sinagua people, who lived and farmed in and around the canyon starting around AD 700. The more than 300 dwellings here were built between 1080 and 1250 and abandoned, like those at so many other settlements in Arizona and New Mexico, around 1300. The Sinagua traded far and wide with other Native Americans, including people at Wupatki. Even macaw feathers, which would have come from tribes in what is now Mexico, have been excavated in the canyon. Early Flagstaff settlers looted the site for pots and "treasure"; Woodrow Wilson declared the site a national monument in 1915, which began a 30-year process of stabilizing the ruins.

Part of the fascination of Walnut Canyon is the opportunity to enter the dwellings, stepping back in time to an ancient way of life. Some of the Sinagua homes are in near-perfect condition in spite of all the looting, because of the dry, hot climate and the protection of overhanging cliffs. You can reach them by descending 185 feet on the 1-mi stepped **Island Trail,** which starts at the visitor center. As you follow the trail, look across the canyon for other dwellings not accessible on the path.

Island Trail takes about an hour to complete at a normal pace. Those with health concerns should opt for the easier ½-mi **Rim Trail,** which has overlooks from which dwell-

The Sinagua

The achievements of the Sinagua people, who lived in north-central Arizona from the 8th through the 15th centuries, reached their height in the 12th and 13th centuries, when related groups occupied most of the San Francisco Volcanic Field and a large portion of the upper and middle Verde Valley. The Sinagua sites around modern-day Camp Verde, Clarkdale, and Flagstaff provide a window into this remarkable culture. Some of the best examples of surviving Sinagua architecture can be found at Walnut Canyon and Wupatki National Monument, northeast of Flagstaff.

ings, as well as an excavated, reconstructed pit house, can be viewed. Picnic areas dot the grounds and line the roads leading to the park. ■TIP➔**Wear layers, as the climate can change quickly.** Guides conduct tours on Wednesday, Saturday, and Sunday from late May through early September. ⊠ *Walnut Canyon Rd., 3 mi south of I–40, Exit 204, Winona* ☎ *928/526–3367* ⊕ *www.nps.gov/waca* ⊠ *$5* ⊙ *Nov.– Apr., daily 9–5; May–Oct., daily 8–5.*

☾ **Meteor Crater,** a natural phenomenon in a privately owned park 43 mi east of Flagstaff, is impressive if for no other reason than its sheer size. A hole in the ground 600 feet deep, nearly 1 mi across, and more than 3 mi in circumference, Meteor Crater is large enough to accommodate the Washington Monument or 20 football fields. It was created by a meteorite crash 49,000 years ago. The area looks so much like the surface of the moon that NASA made it one of the official training sites for the Project Apollo astronauts. You can't descend into the crater because of the efforts of its owners to maintain its condition—scientists consider this to be the best-preserved crater on earth—but guided rim tours, given every hour on the hour from 9 to 3, give useful background information. There's a small snack bar, and the Rock Shop sells specimens from the area and jewelry made from native stones. Take Interstate 40 east of Flagstaff to Exit 233, then drive 6 mi south on Meteor Crater Road. ⊠ *Meteor Crater Rd., 43 mi east of Flagstaff* ☎ *928/289–5898 or 800/289–5898* ⊕ *www.meteorcrater. com* ⊠ *$15* ⊙ *Memorial Day–Labor Day, daily 7–7; Labor Day–Memorial Day, daily 8–5.*

SAN FRANCISCO VOLCANIC FIELD

The San Francisco Volcanic Field north of Flagstaff encompasses 2,000 square mi of fascinating geological phenomena, including ancient volcanoes, cinder cones, valleys carved by water and ice, and the San Francisco Peaks themselves, some of which soar to almost 13,000 feet. There are also some of the most extensive Native American ruins in the Southwest: don't miss Sunset Crater and Wupatki. These national monuments can be explored in relative solitude during much of the year. ■TIP➔The area Is short on services, so fill up on gas and consider taking a picnic.

★ **Sunset Crater Volcano National Monument** lies 14 mi northeast of Flagstaff off U.S. 89. Sunset Crater, a cinder cone that rises 1,000 feet, was an active volcano 900 years ago. Its final eruption contained iron and sulfur, which give the rim of the crater its glow and thus its name. You can walk around the base, but you can't descend into the huge, fragile cone. The **Lava Flow Trail**, a half-hour, mile-long, self-guided walk, provides a good view of the evidence of the volcano's fiery power: lava formations and holes in the rock where volcanic gases vented to the surface.

If you're interested in hiking a volcano, head to **Lenox Crater**, about 1 mi east of the visitor center, and climb the 280 feet to the top of the cinder cone. The cinder is soft and crumbly so wear closed, sturdy shoes. From **O'Leary Peak**, 5 mi from the visitor center on Forest Route 545A, great views can be had of the San Francisco Peaks, the Painted Desert, and beyond. The road is unpaved and rutted, though, so it's advisable to take only high-clearance vehicles, especially in winter. In addition, there's a gate, about halfway along the route, which is usually closed, and when it is, it means a steep 2½-mi hike to the top on foot. To get to the area from Flagstaff, take Santa Fe Avenue east to U.S. 89, and head north for 12 mi; turn right onto the road marked Sunset Crater and go another 2 mi to the visitor center. ⊠*Sunset Crater–Wupatki Loop Rd., 14 mi northeast of Flagstaff* ☎*928/556–0502* ⊕*www.nps.gov/sucr* ⊠*$5, including Wupatki National Monument and Doney Mountain* ⊙*Nov.–Apr., daily 9–5; May–Oct., daily 8–5.*

★ Families from the Sinagua and other ancestral Puebloans are believed to have lived together in harmony on the site that is now **Wupatki National Monument,** farming and trading with one another and with those who passed through. The eruption of Sunset Crater may have influenced migration to this area a century after the event, as freshly laid volcanic cinders held in moisture needed for crops. Although there's evidence of earlier habitation, most of the settlers moved here around 1100 and left the pueblo by about 1250. The 2,700 identified sites contain archaeological evidence of a Native American settlement.

The site for which the national monument was named, the Wupatki (meaning "tall house" in Hopi), was originally three stories high, built above an unexplored system of underground fissures. The structure had almost 100 rooms and an open ball court—evidence of Southwestern trade with Mesoamerican tribes for whom ball games were a central ritual. Next to the ball court is a blowhole, a geologic phenomenon in which air is forced upward by underground pressure.

Other ruins to visit are Wukoki, Lomaki, and the Citadel, a pueblo on a knoll above a limestone sink. Although the largest remnants of Native American settlements at Wupatki National Monument are open to the public, other sites are off-limits. If you're interested in an in-depth tour, consider a ranger-led overnight hike to the **Crack-in-Rock Ruin.** The 14-mi (round-trip) trek covers areas marked by ancient petroglyphs and dotted with well-preserved ruins. The trips are conducted in April and October; call by February or August if you'd like to take part in the lottery for one of the 100 available places on these $50 hikes. Between the Wupatki and Citadel ruins, the **Doney Mountain** affords 360-degree views of the Painted Desert and the San Francisco Volcanic Field. It's a perfect spot for a sunset picnic. In summer, rangers give lectures. ⊠ *Sunset Crater–Wupatki Loop Rd., 19 mi north of Sunset Crater visitor center* ☎ *928/679–2365* ⊕ *www.nps.gov/wupa* ☜ *$5, including Wupatki National Monument and Doney Mountain* ☉ *Daily 9–5.*

CAMERON TRADING POST

54 mi north of Flagstaff on U.S. 89, 67 mi east of Grand Canyon Village on AZ 64.

If you're heading to the Eastern Entrance on the South Rim or to the North Rim via U.S. 89 from Flagstaff and points south, **Cameron Trading Post** on the Navajo Indian Reservation is a worthwhile stop along the way. Most of the jewelry, rugs, baskets, and pottery sold here are made by Navajo and Hopi artisans, but some are created by New Mexico's Zuni and Pueblo Indians. Come armed with knowledge of Native American artisanship if you're looking at high-ticket items, some of which are sold at a separate gallery. Also at the post are a restaurant, cafeteria, grocery store, butcher shop, and post office. An outlet of the **Navajo Arts and Crafts Enterprises** (⊠*AZ 64/U.S. 89* ☎*928/679–2244*) stocks authentic Navajo products.

WHERE TO STAY & EAT

★ **Fodor's**Choice ⊞**Cameron Trading Post.** Fifty-four miles north
$$$ of Flagstaff, this trading post dates back to 1916. Southwestern-style rooms have carved-oak furniture, tile baths, and balconies overlooking the Little Colorado River. Native-stone landscaping—including fossilized dinosaur tracks—and a small, well-kept garden are pleasant. Make your reservations far in advance for high season. The dining room's (¢–$$) delicious homemade green chili and fry bread, Navajo tacos, and hamburgers are alone worth the stop. ⊠*U.S. 89* ⊕*Box 339, Cameron 86020* ☎*928/679–2231 or 800/338–7385 Ext. 414* ☎*928/679–2350* ⊕*www.camerontradingpost.com* ⤳*62 rooms, 4 suites* ⚭*In-hotel: restaurant, public Wi-Fi, no elevator* ☐*AE, DC, MC, V.*

¢ ⚠**Cameron RV Park.** This park, open year-round, is adjacent to the Cameron Trading Post. There are 36 spaces with hookups for $15 a day. However, there are no public restrooms or showers. No reservations accepted. ⊠*U.S. 89* ⊕*Box 339, Cameron 86020* ☎*928/679–2231 or 800/338–7385* ☎*928/679–2350* ⊕*www.camerontradingpost.com* ⤳*36 RV sites* ⚭*Full hookups, dump station, drinking water, food service, general store* ☉*Open year-round.*

EN ROUTE. The route north from Cameron Trading Post on U.S. 89 offers a stunning view of the desert to the right. The desert, which covers thousands of square miles and stretches to the south and east, is a vision of subtle, almost harsh beauty, with windswept plains and mesas, isolated buttes, and barren valleys in pastel patterns. The sparse vegetation is mostly desert scrub, which provides sustenance for only the hardiest wildlife. Most of the undulating hills belong to the 200-million-year-old Chinle formation, the depository of countless fossil records. About 30 mi north of Cameron Trading Post, the desert gives

6

way to sandstone cliffs that run for miles to the right. Brilliantly hued and ranging in color from light pink to deep orange, the **Echo Cliffs** rise to more than 1,000 feet in many places. They are essentially devoid of vegetation, but in a few places high up, thick patches of tall cottonwood and poplar trees, nurtured by springs and water seepage from the rock escarpment, manage to thrive. At Bitter Springs, 60 mi north of Cameron, U.S. 89A branches off U.S. 89, running north and providing views of **Marble Canyon**, the geographical beginning of the Grand Canyon. Like the Grand Canyon, Marble Canyon was formed by the Colorado River. Traversing a gorge nearly 500 feet deep is **Navajo Bridge**, a narrow steel span built in 1929 and listed on the National Register of Historic Places. Formerly used for car traffic, it now functions only as a pedestrian overpass. The visitor center is informational and handy.

LEES FERRY AREA

76 mi north of Cameron Trading Post, U.S. 89 to U.S. 89A.

★ A turnoff at Marble Canyon Lodge, about 200 or 300 yards past Navajo Bridge in the small town of Marble Canyon, leads to historic **Lees Ferry,** 5 mi away. On a sharp bend in the Colorado River where Echo Cliffs and Vermilion Cliffs intersect, Lees Ferry is considered "mile zero" of the river—the point from which all distances on the rivers system in the Grand Canyon are measured.

This spot, one of the last areas in the mainland United States to be completely charted, was first visited by non–Native Americans in 1776, when Spanish priests Fray Francisco Atanasio Domínguez and Fray Silvestre Velez de Escalante tried, but failed, to cross the Colorado. In March 1864, Mormon frontiersman and missionary Jacob Hamblin made the first crossing by raft. Efforts by the Mormons to establish colonies in the area generated high ferry traffic in the 1870s through the 1890s. It became part of the Honeymoon Trail, a gateway to Utah for young couples who wanted their civil marriages in Arizona sanctified at the Latter-day Saints temple in St. George. The ferry also became a crossing and a supply point for miners and other pioneers who shaped the American West. Its most infamous ferryman was John Doyle Lee, who tended the crossing for years before he was arrested and finally executed in connection with the Mountain Meadows massacre in Utah. The ferry was operational until 1928, when a bridge was finally built to span the river.

Lees Ferry retains vestiges of the mining era, but it's now primarily known as the spot where most of the Grand Canyon river rafts put into the water. Huge trout lurk in the river near here, so there are several places to pick up angling gear and a guide.

★ West from the town of Marble Canyon are the spectacular **Vermilion Cliffs,** in many places more than 3,000 feet high. Keep an eye out for condors; the giant endangered birds were reintroduced into the area in the winter of 1996–97. Reports suggest that the birds, once in captivity, are surviving well in the wilderness.

SPORTS & THE OUTDOORS

FISHING

This stretch of ice-cold, crystal-clear water provides arguably the best trout fishing in the Southwest. Many rafters and fishermen stay the night in a campground near the river or in nearby Marble Canyon before hitting the river at dawn. Marble Canyon Lodge sells Arizona fishing licenses. **Lees Ferry Anglers** (⌑*Milepost 547, N. U.S. 89A, Marble Canyon* ☎*928/355–2261, 800/962–9755 outside Arizona* ⊕*www.leesferry.com*) operates guided fishing trips, starting from $350 per day ($435 per day for 2 people); it practices year-round catch and release.

RAFTING

Sixteen companies currently offer excursions, but reservations for raft trips (excluding smooth-water, one-day cruises) often need to be made more than six months in advance. A complete list of concessionaires offering trips on the Colorado River is available on the Grand Canyon National Park Web site (⊕ www.nps.gov/grca). National Park Service white-water concessionaires include Arizona River Runners, Canyoneers, Diamond River Adventures, Grand Canyon Expeditions, and Tour West. For a smooth-water, one-day trip check out Wilderness River Adventures. Prices for river-raft trips vary greatly, depending on type and length. Half-day trips on smooth water run as low as $54 per person. Trips that negotiate the entire length of the canyon and take as long as 16 days can cost more than $200 per day.

Arizona Raft Adventures (✉*4050 E. Huntington Rd., Flagstaff 86004* ☎*928/526–8200 or 800/786–7238* 📠*928/526–8246* ⊕*www.azraft.com*) organizes 6- to 14-day combination paddle-and-oar trips, all paddle, and all motor trips for all skill levels. Trips, which run $1,800 to $3,600, depart from April through October. With a reputation for high quality and a roster of 3- to 14-day trips, **Canyoneers** (✉*Box 2997, Flagstaff 86003* ☎*928/526–0924 or 800/525–0924* 📠*928/527–9398* ⊕*www.canyoneers.com*) is popular with those who want to include some hiking as well. The five-day "Best of the Grand" includes a hike down to Phantom Ranch. Their 3- to 14-day trips, available mid-April through mid-September, cost between $895 and $3,250. Owned and operated by a mother-and-daughters team, **Diamond River Adventures** (✉*Box 1300, Page 86040* ☎*928/645–8866 or 800/343–3121* 📠*928/645–9536* ⊕*www.diamondriver.com*) offers both oar-powered and motorized river trips from 4 to 14 days from May through September. Prices range from $990 to $3,300. Expert and long-established **Grand Canyon Expeditions** (✉*Box O, Kanab, UT 84741* ☎*435/644–2691 or 800/544–2691* 📠*435/644–2699* ⊕*www.gcex.com*) has guided the likes of the Smithsonian Institution along the Colorado River. You can count on them to take you down the river safely and in style: they limit the number of people on each boat to 14, and evening meals might include filet mignon, pork chops, or shrimp. The April through mid-September trips cost $2,300 to $3,500 for 8 to 16 days.

WHERE TO STAY & EAT

¢–$$ 🏨**Marble Canyon Lodge.** This lodge opened in 1929 on the
★   same day the Navajo Bridge was dedicated. Three types of accommodations are available: rooms in the original building; standard motel rooms in the newer building; and two-bedroom apartments. You can sit on the porch of the lodge and look out on Vermilion Cliffs and Echo Cliffs. Zane Grey and Gary Cooper are among the well-known past guests. The restaurant ($–$$$) serves steaks, seafood, pasta, and sandwiches. ✉*¼ mi west of Navajo Bridge on U.S. 89A* ✉*Box 6001, Marble Canyon 86036* ☎*928/355–2225 or 800/726–1789* 📠*928/355–2227* 🛏*52 units* 🍴*In-*

hotel: restaurant, bar, laundry facilities, some pets allowed ⊐*AE, D, MC, V.*

¢–$ ⊡**Cliff Dwellers Lodge.** Built in 1949, this dining and lodging complex sits at the foot of Vermilion Cliffs. Rooms in the modern motel building are attractive and clean. **Lees Ferry Anglers** (☎*928/355–2261 or 800/962–9755 ⊕www. leesferry.com*) is headquartered at this lodge, adding to the convenience of a fly-fishing trip on the Colorado River. ⊠*U.S. 89A, 9 mi west of Navajo Bridge* ⌂*HC 67, Box 30, Marble Canyon 86036* ☎*928/355–2228 or 800/433–2543* ↪*22 rooms* ⌂*In-hotel: restaurant, bar, some pets allowed (fee)* ⊐*AE, D, MC, V.*

¢–$ ⊡**Lees Ferry Lodge.** At the end of the day you can sit out on one of the garden patios of this rustic 1929 building. Rooms are charming, if a bit quirky in their plumbing. The hotel's Vermilion Cliffs Bar and Grill ($–$$$) is a popular gathering spot for river raft guides, and serves good American fare—especially steaks and ribs—in an authentic Western setting. The bar has an extensive beer collection: 92 types so far. ⊠*4 mi west of Navajo Bridge on U.S. 89A* ⌂*HC 67, Box 1, Marble Canyon 86036* ☎*928/355–2231 or 800/451–2231 ⊕www.leesferrylodge.com* ↪*11 rooms, 3 5-person trailers* ⌂*In-room: no phone, no TV (some), refrigerator. In-hotel: restaurant, bar* ⊐*AE, MC, V.*

EN ROUTE. As you continue the journey to the North Rim, the immense blue-green bulk of the Kaibab Plateau stretches out before you. About 18 mi past Navajo Bridge, a sign directs you to the **San Bartolome Historic Site,** an overlook with plaques that tell the story of the Domínguez-Escalante expedition of 1776. At **House Rock Valley,** a large road sign announces the House Rock Buffalo Ranch, operated by the Arizona Game and Fish Department. A 23-mi dirt road leads to the home of one of the largest herds of American bison in the Southwest. You can drive out to the ranch, but you might not see any buffalo—the expanse of their range is so great that they frequently cannot be spotted from a car. As it nears its junction with AZ 67, U.S. 89A starts climbing to the top of the **Kaibab Plateau,** heavily forested, filled with animals and birds, and more than 9,000 feet at its highest point. The rapid change from barren desert to lush forest is dramatic.

JACOB LAKE

25 mi west of town of Marble Canyon on U.S. 89A, at AZ 67.

Jacob Lake junction is a good base camp for exploring the beautiful Kaibab Plateau. The Kaibab squirrel—a sub-species of the tassel-eared squirrel found only in this region—is one of the many species of wildlife encountered here.

The U.S. Forest Service's **Kaibab Plateau Visitor's Center** (⊠ *U. S. 89A/AZ 67* ☎*928/643–7298* ⊕*www.fs.fed.us/r3/kai*) is open May–mid-October and has several interpretive displays, books, and educational gifts. Gas and groceries are also available in the area.

WHERE TO STAY & EAT

¢–$$ 🏨 **Jacob Lake Inn.** The bustling lodge at Jacob Lake Inn is a popular stop for those heading to the North Rim; it has a grocery store, coffee shop, restaurant (¢–$), and gift shop. Even if you don't stay here, stop for one of their famous malts or milk shakes. The 5-acre complex in Kaibab National Forest has basic cabins and standard motel rooms that overlook the forest. Twenty-five rooms added in 2006 have TVs, phones, Wi-Fi, and in-room broadband. ⊠*AZ 67/U.S. 89A, 86022* ☎*928/643–7232* ⊕*www.jacoblake. com* ➪*39 rooms, 22 cabins* ₼*In-room: no a/c (some), no phone (some), no TV (some), dial-up (some), Wi-Fi (some). In-hotel: restaurant* ⊟*AE, D, MC, V.*

CAMPING

¢ ⛺ **DeMotte Campground.** Surrounded by tall pines, this U.S. Forest Service campground is 38 mi south of Jacob Lake. It has 23 single-unit (RV or tent) sites but no hookups, for $17 per day. There are interpretive campfire programs in summer. ⊠*Off AZ 67* ⚑*North Kaibab Ranger District, Box 248, Fredonia 86022* ☎*928/643–7395* ➪*38 campsites* ₼*Flush toilets, fire pits, picnic tables* ⚑*Reservations not accepted* ☉*Open mid-May–mid-Oct.*

¢ ⛺ **Kaibab Camper Village.** Fire pits and more than 70 picnic tables are spread out in this wooded spot, which is near a gas station, store, and restaurant. Reservations are accepted by the Canyoneers outfitter and are recommended, particularly during the height of the busy summer season. There are 20 tent sites ($17 for two people) and 60 RV and trailer sites ($33 for a pull-through with full hookup, $13 without hookup). ⊠*AZ 67, ¼ mi south of U.S. 89A* ☐*Box 3331, Flagstaff 86003* ☎*928/643–7804 in season, 928/526–0924, 800/525–0924 outside AZ in winter* 🖷*928/527–9398* ⊕*www.kaibabcampervillage.com* ⇆*60 full hookups, 50 tent sites* ⚠*Portable toilets, full hookups, laundry facilities, drinking water, showers, fire pits, picnic tables* ⊙*Open mid-May–mid-Oct.*

EN ROUTE. AZ 67 runs south from U.S. 89A to the North Rim; the route passes through one of the thickest stands of ponderosa pine in the United States. You'll see mule deer and Kaibab squirrels. Keep an eye out for mountain lions ... they're here, but seeing them is rare. You're more likely to see wild turkeys.

ELSEWHERE IN THE ARIZONA STRIP

The Arizona Strip—the part of the state directly north of Grand Canyon National Park—has only two small towns, Fredonia and Colorado City. The combined population of these two towns is less than 6,000, and fewer than 700 permanent residents—including 150 members of the Kaibab-Paiute tribe—live in the rest of the strip. There are no facilities or services of any kind once you leave the highway; top off your tank when you find a gas station, and keep an ample supply of drinking water in your car. Away from the paved highways in this region, roads tend to be rough and may be impassable when wet.

★ **Fodor's**Choice **Pipe Spring National Monument,** 90 mi from the North Rim and 14 mi from Fredonia, has one of the few reliable sources of water in the Arizona Strip. The park contains a restored rock fort and ranch, with exhibits of Southwestern frontier life. In summer there are living-history demonstrations of ranching operations or weaving. The fort was intended to fend off Native American attacks (which never came because a peace treaty was signed before the fort was finished). It ended up functioning mainly as headquarters for a dairy and ranching operation and in 1871 became the first telegraph station in the Arizona Territory. About ½ mi north of the monument is a campground and picnic area operated by the Kaibab-Paiute tribe. Check out the museum and visitor center, which is operated jointly by the tribe and the National Park Service. ⊠*401 N. Pipe Spring Rd.* ☐*HC 65, Box 5, Fredonia 86022* ☎*928/643–7105* ⊕*www.nps.gov/pisp* ⊠*$4*

⊙*Historic structure,s daily 8:30–4:30; visitor center and museum, Sept.–May, daily 8–5; June–Aug., daily 7–5.*

Six miles back toward Fredonia from Pipe Spring on AZ 389, a dirt road leads 50 mi south through starkly beautiful, uninhabited country to **Toroweap Overlook,** a lonely and awesome viewpoint over one of the narrowest stretches of the Grand Canyon (less than 1 mi across). The overlook has the deepest sheer cliff (more than 3,000 feet straight down) in the Grand Canyon. From this vantage point, you can see upstream to sedimentary ledges, cliffs, and talus slopes. Looking downstream, you can see miles of the lava flow that forms steep deltas, some of which look like black waterfalls frozen on the cliff. Be sure you have plenty of gas, drinking water, good tires, and a reliable car; a high-clearance vehicle is best for this trip. It's a rough drive, especially the last 3 mi over slickrock. Allow up to three hours to drive from the highway to the overlook. Don't try to go in wet weather, when the dirt road is likely to be washed out. There's a ranger station near the rim as well as a primitive campground, which has 11 first-come, first-served tent sites, picnic tables, grates, and compost toilets but no drinking water. If you plan to return the same day, make motel reservations in advance at an Arizona Strip motel.

Grand Canyon National Park Essentials

There are planners and there are those who, excuse the pun, fly by the seat of their pants. We happily place ourselves among the planners. Our writers and editors try to anticipate all the issues you may face before and during any journey, and then they do their research. This section is the product of their efforts. Use it to get excited about your trip to Grand Canyon National Park, to inform your travel planning, or to guide you on the road should the seat of your pants start to feel threadbare.

www.fodors.com/forums

GETTING STARTED

We're very proud of our Web site: Fodors.com is a great place to begin any journey. Scan "Travel Wire" for suggested itineraries, travel deals, restaurant and hotel openings, and other up-to-the-minute info. Check out "Booking" to research prices and book plane tickets, hotel rooms, rental cars, and vacation packages. Head to "Talk" for on-the-ground pointers from travelers who frequent our message boards. You can also link to loads of other travel-related resources.

▌RESOURCES

ONLINE TRAVEL TOOLS
For more specific information on the Grand Canyon, visit the following Web sites.

ALL ABOUT THE GRAND CANYON
The site for the **National Park Service** (⊕*www.nps.gov*) has links to the several national parks in Arizona. You can find out much more about the park at **The Canyon** (⊕*www.thecanyon.com*).

Safety Transportation Security Administration (TSA; ⊕www.tsa.gov).

Time Zones Timeanddate.com (⊕www.timeanddate.com/world clock) can help you figure out the correct time anywhere.

Weather Accuweather.com (⊕www.accuweather.com) is an independent weather-forecasting service with good coverage of hurricanes. **Weather.com** (⊕www.weather.com) is the Web site for the Weather Channel.

VISITOR INFORMATION
Tourist Information Arizona Office of Tourism (☎602/364–3700 or 866/275–5816 ⊕www.arizona guide.com).

Native American Resources Havasupai Tourist Enterprise (☎928/448–2141 ⊕www.havasu paitribe.com). **Navajo Nation Tourism Office** (☎928/871–6436 ⊕www.discovernavajo.com).

▌THINGS TO CONSIDER

ACCESSIBILITY
The historic buildings in Grand Canyon National Park were built before handicap accessibility became commonplace. Accessible lodging on the South Rim includes El Tovar, Thunderbird Lodge, Kachina Lodge, Yavapai Lodge, and Maswik Lodge. Handicap-accessible restrooms can be found at the Bright Angel Lodge, El Tovar (request key at the front desk), Maswik Lodge, Backcountry Information Center at the Maswik Transportation Center, Canyon View Information Plaza, Yavapai Observation Station, Tusayan Ruin and Museum, Desert View, and the Shrine of Ages.

Accessible shuttle buses are not available without a 24-hour advance reservation (☎ 928/638–0591). However, special permits can be obtained for private vehicles on Hermit Road. On the North Rim, the Grand Canyon Lodge offers a few accessible rooms and a limited access restroom. The North Rim Visitor Center and the North Rim Campground both have handicap-accessible restrooms. Wheelchairs are available for temporary day use and can be picked up at the Canyon View Information Plaza on the South Rim and at the Grand Canyon Lodge on the North Rim.

ADMISSION FEES

Admission fees for entrance to Grand Canyon National Park are $25 per vehicle and $12 per person for pedestrians and cyclists. The fees are collected at the east entrance near Cameron and at the south entrance near Tusayan for the South Rim and at the main entrance at the North Rim. The fee pays for up to one week's access and is good for both rims. The Grand Canyon Pass, available for $50, gives unlimited access to the park for 12 months from the purchase date. The America the Beautiful—National Parks and Recreational Lands Pass, available for $80, gives unlimited access to all federal recreation areas and national parks for 12 months from purchase date. The America the Beautiful Senior Pass has the same benefits for U.S. citizens age 62 or older for the cost of $10.

All visitors (except Native Americans with a valid tribal ID) entering the Havasu Indian Reservation are required to pay an entrance fee: $35 for adults and $17.50 for children 12 and under. Visitors are also required to pay a $5 per person environmental-care fee. This fee will be refunded to all visitors carrying a bag of garbage back out of the canyon. Entrance fees are to be paid upon arrival at the tribal tourism office. Admission fees to Hualapai Reservation are included in the Grand Canyon West tour packages.

ADMISSION HOURS

The South Rim is open 24/7, year-round. The North Rim is open mid-May through mid-October, depending on the weather. Highway 67 from Jacob Lake is closed due to snowfall from around mid-November to mid-May, and during these times all facilities at the North Rim are closed. The entrance gates are open 24 hours, but are generally staffed from about 7 AM to 7 PM. If you arrive when there's no one at the gate, you may enter legally without paying. The park is in the mountain standard time zone year-round. Daylight savings time is not observed.

PERMITS

Hikers descending into the canyon for an overnight stay need a backcountry permit ($10, plus $5 per person per night), which can be obtained in person, by mail, or faxed by request. Permits are limited, so make your reservation as far in advance as possible (they're taken up to four months ahead of arrival). A visit to the park's Web site will go far in preparing you for the permit process. Day hikes into the canyon or anywhere else in the national park do not require a permit; overnight stays at Phantom Ranch require reservations but no permits. Overnight camping in the national park is restricted to designated campgrounds.

The North Rim may be accessed in the winter by hiking, cross-country skiing, or snowshoeing. Winter visitors must obtain a backcountry permit for overnight use during the winter season (later October through mid-May). Between the North Kaibab trailhead and Bright Angel Point, all overnight visitors are required to stay at the North Rim Campground. Winter campers can camp-at-large at all other areas between the northern boundary and the North Kaibab trailhead.

Information Backcountry Information Center (Box 129, Grand Canyon 86023 928/638-7875 928/638-2125 www.nps.com/grca).

TRIP INSURANCE

What kind of coverage do you honestly need? Do you even need trip insurance at all? Take a deep breath and read on.

We believe that comprehensive trip insurance is especially valuable if you're booking a very expensive or complicated trip (particularly to an isolated region) or if you're booking far

in advance. Who knows what could happen six months down the road? But whether or not you get insurance has more to do with how comfortable you are assuming all that risk yourself.

Comprehensive travel policies typically cover trip-cancellation and interruption, letting you cancel or cut your trip short because of a personal emergency, illness, or, in some cases, acts of terrorism in your destination. Such policies also cover evacuation and medical care. Some also cover you for trip delays because of bad weather or mechanical problems as well as for lost or delayed baggage. Another type of coverage to look for is financial default—that is, when your trip is disrupted because a tour operator, airline, or cruise line goes out of business. Generally you must buy this when you book your trip or shortly thereafter, and it's only available to you if your operator isn't on a list of excluded companies.

Expect comprehensive travel-insurance policies to cost about 4% to 7% of the total price of your trip (it's more like 12% if you're over age 70). A medical-only policy may or may not be cheaper than a comprehensive policy. Always read the fine print of your policy to make sure that you are covered for the risks that are of most concern to you. Compare several policies to make sure you're getting the best price and range of coverage available.

Trip-Insurance Resources

INSURANCE COMPARISON SITES		
Insure My Trip.com	800/487–4722	www.insuremytrip.com
Square Mouth.com	800/240–0369	www.quotetravelinsurance.com
COMPREHENSIVE TRAVEL INSURERS		
Access America	866/807–3982	www.accessamerica.com
CSA Travel Protection	800/873–9855	www.csatravelprotection.com
HTH Worldwide	610/254–8700 or 888/243–2358	www.hthworldwide.com
Travelex Insurance	888/457–4602	www.travelex-insurance.com '
Travel Guard International	715/345–0505 or 800/826–4919	www.travelguard.com
Travel Insured International	800/243–3174	www.travelinsured.com
MEDICAL-ONLY INSURERS		
International Medical Group	800/628–4664	www.imglobal.com
International SOS	215/942–8000 or 713/521–7611	www.internationalsos.com
Wallach & Company	800/237–6615 or 504/687–3166	www.wallach.com

BOOKING YOUR TRIP

Unless your cousin is a travel agent, you're probably among the millions of people who make most of their travel arrangements online.

But have you ever wondered just what the differences are between an online travel agent (a Web site through which you make reservations instead of going directly to the airline, hotel, or car-rental company), a discounter (a firm that does a high volume of business with a hotel chain or airline and accordingly gets good prices), a wholesaler (one that makes cheap reservations in bulk and then re-sells them to people like you), and an aggregator (one that compares all the offerings so you don't have to)?

Is it truly better to book directly on an airline or hotel Web site? And when does a real live travel agent come in handy?

▌ONLINE

You really have to shop around. A travel wholesaler such as Hotels.com or HotelClub.net can be a source of good rates, as can discounters such as Hotwire or Priceline, particularly if you can bid for your hotel room or airfare. Indeed, such sites sometimes have deals that are unavailable elsewhere. They do, however, tend to work only with hotel chains (which makes them just plain useless for getting hotel reservations outside of major cities) or big airlines (so that often leaves out upstarts like jetBlue and some foreign carriers like Air India).

Also, with discounters and wholesalers you must generally prepay, and everything is non-refundable. And before you fork over the dough, be sure to check the terms and conditions, so you know what a given company will do for you if there's a problem and what you'll have to deal with on your own.

■TIP→ **To be absolutely sure everything was processed correctly, confirm reservations made through online travel agents, discounters, and wholesalers directly with your hotel before leaving home.**

Booking engines like Expedia, Travelocity, and Orbitz are actually travel agents, albeit high-volume, online ones. And airline travel packagers like American Airlines Vacations and Virgin Vacations—well, they're travel agents, too. But they may still not work with all the world's hotels.

An aggregator site will search many sites and pull the best prices for airfares, hotels, and rental cars from them. Most aggregators compare the major travel-booking sites such as Expedia, Travelocity, and Orbitz; some also look at airline Web sites, though rarely the sites of smaller budget airlines. Some aggregators also compare other travel products, including complex packages—a good thing, as you can sometimes get the best overall deal by booking an air-and-hotel package.

I ACCOMMODATIONS

Grand Canyon in-park lodgings range from three historic but rustic hotels to simple cabins to bland modern motels. The few frills will be found at the El Tovar, which is also the most expensive lodging inside the park—but even there frills are hard to find, the best in-room amenity being a view of the canyon (and not all rooms at El Tovar offer that). Although prices vary widely, most rooms are between $100 and $150.

Reservations are absolutely essential at the Grand Canyon if you want to stay in the park. Reservations are taken 13 months in advance, and you need to plan far ahead to stay in Bright Angel Lodge, El Tovar, or the Grand Canyon Lodge at the North Rim. Cancellations are common, so if you don't find a room the first time you check, keep trying. You may even find a last-minute cancellation, but don't count on it. With short notice, the best time to find a room at the South Rim is during winter. Although the North Rim is less crowded than the South Rim, rooms are limited and available only from mid-May through mid-October. If you still can't find a room, you could also consider booking a train excursion through the Grand Canyon Railway, which leaves from Williams; some packages include an overnight stay in the park, and these packages are sometimes available even at short notice.

Just outside the park, Tusayan's hotels offer a convenient location but no bargains, while Williams and Flagstaff can provide much cheaper prices on food and lodging, as well as a respite from the crowds. However, you must contend with the distance, and if you are staying more than a single night, that should be a serious consideration.

The lodgings we list are the cream of the crop in each price category. We always list the facilities that are available, but we don't specify whether they cost extra, when pricing accommodations, always ask what's included and what costs extra. Properties are assigned price categories based on the range from their least-expensive standard double room at high season (excluding holidays) to the most expensive. Properties marked ✕⊞ are lodging establishments whose restaurants warrant a special trip. A price chart appears at the start of each chapter.

Most hotels and other lodgings require your credit-card details before they will confirm your reservation. If you don't feel comfortable e-mailing this

Online-Booking Resources

AGGREGATORS		
Kayak	www.kayak.com	also looks at cruises and vacation packages.
Mobissimo	www.mobissimo. com	
Qixo	www.qixo.com	also compares cruises, vacation packages, and even travel insurance.
Sidestep	www.sidestep. com	also compares vacation packages and lists travel deals.
Travelgrove	www.travelgrove. com	also compares cruises and packages.

BOOKING ENGINES		
Cheap Tickets	www.cheap tickets.com	a discounter.
Expedia	www.expedia. com	a large online agency that charges a booking fee for airline tickets.
Hotwire	www.hotwire.com	a discounter.
lastminute.com	www.lastminute. com	specializes in last-minute travel; the main site is for the U.K., but it has a link to a U.S. site.
Luxury Link	www.luxurylink. com	has auctions (surprisingly good deals) as well as offers on the high-end side of travel.
Onetravel.com	www.onetravel. com	a discounter for hotels, car rentals, airfares, and packages.
Orbitz	www.orbitz.com	charges a booking fee for airline tickets, but gives a clear breakdown of fees and taxes before you book.
Priceline.com	www.priceline. com	a discounter that also allows bidding.
Travel.com	www.travel.com	allows you to compare its rates with those of other booking engines.
Travelocity	www.travelocity. com	charges a booking fee for airline tickets, but promises good problem resolution.

Online-Booking Resources

Hotelbook.com	www.hotelbook.com	focuses on independent hotels worldwide.
Hotel Club	www.hotelclub.net	good for major cities worldwide.
Hotels.com	www.hotels.com	a big Expedia-owned wholesaler that offers rooms in hotels all over the world.
Quikbook	www.quikbook.com	offers "pay when you stay" reservations that let you settle your bill at check out, not when you book.
OTHER RESOURCES		
Bidding For Travel	www.biddingfortravel.com	a good place to figure out what you can get and for how much before you start bidding on, say, Priceline.

information, ask if you can fax it (some places even prefer faxes). However you book, get confirmation in writing and have a copy handy when you check in.

Be sure you understand the hotel's cancellation policy. Some places allow you to cancel without any kind of penalty—even if you prepaid to secure a discounted rate—if you cancel at least 24 hours in advance. Others require you to cancel a week in advance or penalize you the cost of one night. Small inns and B&Bs are most likely to require you to cancel far in advance. Most hotels allow children under a certain age to stay in their parents' room at no extra charge, but others charge for them as extra adults; find out the cutoff age for discounts.

■TIP→Assume that hotels operate on the European Plan (EP, no meals) unless we specify that they use the Breakfast Plan (BP, with full breakfast), Continental Plan (CP, continental breakfast), Full American Plan (FAP, all meals), Modified American Plan (MAP, breakfast and dinner) or are all-inclusive (AI, all meals and most activities).

▌AIRLINE TICKETS

Most domestic airline tickets are electronic; international tickets may be either electronic or paper. With an e-ticket the only thing you receive is an e-mailed receipt citing your itinerary and reservation and ticket numbers.

The greatest advantage of an e-ticket is that if you lose your receipt, you can simply print out another copy or ask the airline to do it for you at check-in. You usually pay a surcharge (up to $50) to get a paper ticket, if you can get one at all.

Car-Rental Resources

AUTOMOBILE ASSOCIATIONS

American Automobile Association	315/797–5000	www.aaa.com; most contact with the organization is through state and regional members
National Automobile Club	650/294–7000	www.thenac.com; membership open to CA residents only

LOCAL AGENCIES

ABC Rent-A-Car	800/773–6814	www.abc-rentacar.com
Arizona Auto Rental	520/624–4548	
Fox Rent A Car	800/225–4369	www.foxrentacar.com

MAJOR AGENCIES

Alamo	800/462–5266	www.alamo.com
Avis	800/331–1084	www.avis.com
Budget	800/472–3325	www.budget.com
Hertz	800/654–3131	www.hertz.com
National Car Rental	800/227–7368	www.nationalcar.com

The sole advantage of a paper ticket is that it may be easier to endorse over to another airline if your flight is canceled and the airline with which you booked can't accommodate you on another flight.

❚ RENTAL CARS

When you reserve a car, ask about cancellation penalties, taxes, drop-off charges (if you're planning to pick up the car in one city and leave it in another), and surcharges (for being under or over a certain age, for additional drivers, or for driving across state or country borders or beyond a specific distance from your point of rental). All these things can add substantially to your costs. Request car seats and extras such as GPS when you book.

Rates are sometimes—but not always—better if you book in advance or reserve through a rental agency's Web site. There are other reasons to book ahead, though: for popular destinations, during busy times of the year, or to ensure that you get certain types of cars (vans, SUVs, exotic sports cars).

■ TIP➔ Make sure that a confirmed reservation guarantees you a car. Agencies sometimes overbook, particularly for busy weekends and holiday periods.

You will almost certainly need a rental car to visit the Grand Canyon. Rates in Arizona begin around $25 a day or $150 a week for an economy car with air-conditioning, automatic transmission, and unlimited mileage. This doesn't include taxes and fees on car rentals, which can range from about 15% to 50%, depending on pickup location. When you add the daily fees, taxes and fees can add up to almost half the cost of the car rental from Phoenix Sky Harbor airport. Elsewhere, taxes are typically around 25% or less.

Rates in Phoenix may be higher during the winter, which is considered high tourist season. Check the Internet or local papers for discounts and deals. Local rental agencies also frequently offer lower rates.

In Arizona most agencies won't rent to you if you're under the age of 21, and several major agencies will not rent to anyone under 25.

CAR-RENTAL INSURANCE

Everyone who rents a car wonders whether the insurance the rental companies offer is worth it. No one—including us—has a simple answer. It depends on how much regular insurance you have, how comfortable you are with risk, and whether money is an issue.

If you own a car and carry comprehensive car insurance for both collision and liability, your personal auto insurance will probably cover a rental, but read your policy's fine print to be sure. If you don't have auto insurance, then you should probably buy the collision- or loss-damage waiver (CDW or LDW) from the rental company. This eliminates your liability for damage to the car.

Some credit cards offer CDW coverage, but it's usually supplemental to your own insurance and rarely covers SUVs, minivans, luxury models, and the like. If your coverage is secondary, you may still be liable for loss-of-use costs from the car-rental company (again, read the fine print). But no credit-card insurance is valid unless you use that card for *all* transactions, from reserving to paying the final bill.

You may also be offered supplemental liability coverage; the car-rental company is required to carry a minimal level of liability coverage insuring all renters, but it's rarely enough to cover claims in a really serious accident if you're at fault. Your own auto-insurance policy will protect you if you own a car; if you don't, you have to decide whether you are willing to take the risk.

U.S. rental companies sell CDWs and LDWs for about $15 to $25 a day; supplemental liability is usually more than $10 a day. The car-rental company may offer you all sorts of other policies, but they're rarely worth the cost. Personal accident insurance, which is basic hospitalization coverage, is an especially egregious rip-off if you already have health insurance.

■TIP➜ **You can decline the insurance from the rental company and purchase it through a third-party provider such as Travel Guard (www.travelguard.com)—$9 per day for $35,000 of coverage. That's sometimes just under half the price of the CDW offered by some car-rental companies.**

In Arizona the car-rental agency's insurance is primary; therefore, the company must pay for damage to third parties up to a preset legal limit, beyond which your own liability insurance kicks in.

▌ SPECIAL-INTEREST TOURS

AIR TOURS

Flights by plane and helicopter over the canyon are offered by a number of companies, departing for the Grand Canyon Airport at the south end of Tusayan. Prices and lengths of tours vary, but you can expect to pay about $109–$120 per adult for short plane trips and approximately $130–$235 for a brief helicopter tour.

Contacts Air Grand Canyon(✉ Grand Canyon Airport, Tusayan ☎928/638—2686 or 800/247–4726 ⊕www.airgrandcanyon. com). **Grand Canyon Airlines** (✉ Grand Canyon Airport, Tusayan ☎928/638–2359 or 866/235–9422 ⊕www.grandcan yonairlines.com). **Grand Canyon Helicopters**(✉ Grand Canyon Airport, Tusayan ☎928/638–2764 or 800/541–4537 ⊕www.grandcan

yonhelicoptersaz.com).**Maverick Helicopters**(✉ Grand Canyon Airport, Tusayan ☎928/638–2622 or 800/962–3869 ⊕www.mav erickhelicopters.com).**Papillon Helicopters**(✉ Grand Canyon Airport, Tusayan ☎928/638–2419 or 800/528–2418 ⊕www.papillon.com).

BUS TOURS

Narrated motorcoach tours on the South Rim cover Hermits Rest Road and Desert View Drive. Other options include sunrise and sunset tours. Prices range from $14.50 to $40 per person. GI id="d2e1987"

Contacts Xanterra Motorcoach Tours(✉ Grand Canyon Village ☎928/638–2631 or 928/638–3283 ⊕www.grandcanyonlodges. com).

HIKING TOURS

The Grand Canyon Field Institute leads a full program of educational guided hikes around the canyon year-round. Topics include everything from archaeology and backcountry medicine to photography and natural history. Reservations are essential and cost from $95 to $795. For a personalized tour of the Grand Canyon and surrounding sacred sites, contact Marvelous Marv, whose knowledge of the area is as extensive as his repertoire of local legends. The National Geographic Visitor Center offers guided hiking and photography tours. Hikes held by Angel's Gate Tours range from "mild" to "extreme" and range in price from $159 to $245.

Contacts Angel's Gate Tours (✉

112 Kletha Trail, Flagstaff, 86001
☎928/814–2277 or 800/957–4557
⊕www.seegrand canyon.com).
Grand Canyon Field Institute
(✉ Box 399, Grand Canyon,
86023 ☎ 928/638–2485 or
866/471–4435 ⊕www.grandcanyon.
org/fieldinstitute).**Marvelous Marv
& Magnificent Maggie's Grand
Canyon Tour** (✉ Box 544, Williams,
86046 ☎ 928/707–0291 ⊕www.
marvelousmarv.com). **National Geographic Visitor Center Grand Canyon** (✉ Hwy 64/U.S. 180, Tusayan
☎ 888/355-0550 ⊕www.explore
thecanyon.com).

JEEP TOURS

If you'd like to get off the pavement and see parts of the South
Rim that are accessible only by
dirt road, a jeep tour can be just
the ticket. Rides can be rough;
if you have had back injuries,
check with your doctor before
taking a jeep tour. Offerings
include trips into the Kaibab
Forest, sunset tours, Old West
tours, inner canyon trips, and
helicopter/jeep combos. Grand
Canyon Old West Jeep Tours
also offers an all-day adventure to the inner canyon on
the Hualapai Reservation. This
trip departs year-round from
Williams and the South Rim's
Grand Canyon Village.

**Contacts Grand Canyon Jeep and
Safari Tours** (✉ Box 1772, Grand
Canyon, 86023 ☎ 928/638–5337
or 800/320–5337 ⊕www.grand
canyonjeeptours.com).**Grand Canyon Old West Jeep Tours** (✉
Grand Canyon ☎928/638–2000 or
866/638–4386 ⊕www.grandcanyon
jeeps.com).

SIGHTSEEING TOURS

It's possible to beat the crowds
with a guided tour of Grand
Canyon National Parks from
Flagstaff or some other nearby
town. Half-day and full day trips
range in price from $60 to $109
per person.

**Contacts American Dream Tours
Inc.** (✉ *Box 2822, Flagstaff,
86004 ☎ 888/203–1212
⊕www.ameri candreamtours.
com).* **Angel's Gate Tours** (✉ *112
Kletha Trail, Flagstaff, 86001
☎928/814–2277 or 800/957–
4557⊕www.seegrandcanyon.
com).* **Discover Grand Canyon**
(✉ *Box 3398, Grand Can-
yon, 86023 ☎928/638–1088
⊕www.discovergrandcanyon
tours.com).*

TRANSPORTATION

▮ BY AIR

While it's possible to fly directly to the Grand Canyon Airport, most visitors fly into one of the region's other airports and make the last leg of the trip by car.

Airlines & Airports Airline and Airport Links.com (⊕www.airlineandairportlinks.com) has links to many of the world's airlines and airports.

Airline Security Issues Transportation Security Administration (⊕www.tsa.gov) has answers for almost every question that might come up.

AIRPORTS

Major gateways to the Grand Canyon include Phoenix Sky Harbor International (PHX), Flagstaff Pulliam Airport (FLG), and even Las Vegas McCarren Airport (LAS) for either the North or South Rim, though St. George Airport (SGU) is the closest.

Phoenix Sky Harbor International Airport is the fifth-busiest airport in the world for take-offs and landings but rarely suffers from congestion or lengthy lines. It's about 220 mi from the South Rim (at least 4 hours travel time).

Flagstaff Pulliam Airport has relatively little scheduled service, all on regional jets. It's about 78 mi from the South Rim.

Las Vegas McCarren Airport is one of the region's busiest airport, but because of that it offers more scheduled flights than any other airport than Phoenix. Still, it's 277 mi from the North Rim and 290 mi from the South Rim.

The closest airport to the North Rim is actually in St. George, UT, 164 mi from the North Rim.

Airport Information Flagstaff Pulliam Airport (☎928/556–1234). **Grand Canyon National Parks Airport** (☎ 928/638–2446).**McCarren International Airport** (☎702/261–5211 ⊕www.mccarren.com).**Phoenix Sky Harbor International** (☎602/273–3300 ⊕www.phxskyharbor.com).**St. George Municipal Airport** (☎435/634–5822 ⊕www.sgcity.org/airport).

FLIGHTS

Phoenix is a hub for Southwest Airlines and US Airways. These carriers offer the most direct flights in and out of Phoenix. Most of the nation's other major airlines also fly into Phoenix.

Among the smaller airlines, ATA flies between Phoenix and New York, Washington, and Hawaii. Frontier connects Phoenix with Denver. Midwest Express connects Phoenix and Milwaukee. JetBlue has service from Phoenix to Boston and New York. Sun Country Airlines flies from Phoenix to Minneapolis.

Within Arizona, US Airways Express/Mesa Airlines (part of US Airways) flies from Phoenix to Flagstaff. Show Low.

All the nation's major carriers have flights to Las Vegas. Several carriers fly to the Grand Canyon Airport from Las Vegas, including Air Vegas, Scenic Airlines, and Vision Holidays.

Airline Contacts Alaska Airlines (☎800/252–7522 or 206/433–3100 ⊕www.alaskaair.com). **American Airlines** (☎800/433–7300 ⊕www. aa.com). **ATA** (☎800/435–9282 or 317/282–8308 ⊕www.ata. com). **Continental Airlines** (☎800/523–3273 for U.S. and Mexico reservations, 800/231–0856 for international reservations ⊕www. continental.com). **Delta Airlines** (☎800/221–1212 for U.S. reservations, 800/241–4141 for international reservations ⊕www.delta. com). **jetBlue** (☎800/538–2583 ⊕www.jetblue.com). **Northwest Airlines** (☎800/225–2525 ⊕www.nwa.com). **Southwest Airlines** (☎800/435–9792 ⊕www. southwest.com). **United Airlines** (☎800/864–8331 for U.S. reservations, 800/538–2929 for international reservations ⊕www.united. com). **USAirways** (☎800/428–4322 for U.S. and Canada reservations, 800/622–1015 for international reservations ⊕www.usairways.com).

Smaller Airlines AeroMexico (☎800/800–9999 ⊕www. aeromexico.com). **Air Vegas** (☎800/940–2550 ⊕www.airvegas.com). **Frontier Airlines** (☎800/432–1359 ⊕www.frontierairlines.com). **Great Lakes Airlines** (☎800/554–5111 ⊕www.greatlakesav.com). **Midwest Express** (☎800/452–2022 ⊕www. midwestexpress.com). **Scenic Airlines** (☎800/634–6801 ⊕www. scenic.com). **Sun Country Airlines** (☎800/359–6786 ⊕www. suncountry.com). **Vision Holidays** (☎702/261–3850 or 800/256–8767 ⊕www.visionholidays.com).

❚ BY BUS

There's no public bus transportation to the Grand Canyon. Greyhound Lines provides bus service to Williams, Flagstaff, and Kingman. Schedules change frequently; call or check the Web site for information. Flagstaff Express Shuttle offers service from Phoenix to Flagstaff and between Flagstaff and Williams to Grand Canyon Village. Open Road Tours offers shuttle service from Flagstaff and Williams to Tusayan and Grand Canyon Village.

On the South Rim of the park, there are three free shuttle routes. Hermits Rest Route operates from March through November between Grand Canyon Village and Hermits Rest; it runs every 15 to 30 minutes one hour before sunrise until one hour after sunset, depending on the season. The Village Route operates year-round in the village area from one hour before sunrise until after dark; it is the easiest access to the Canyon View Information Center. The Kaibab Trail Route travels from Canyon View Information Center to Yaki

Point, including a stop at the South Kaibab Trailhead.

The North Rim offers a shuttle to the North Kaibab Trailhead twice a day. Fees are $7 for the first person and $4 for each additional person in the group. Reservations are required 24 hours in advance and are available for purchase at the Grand Canyon Lodge front desk.

From mid-May to late October, the Trans Canyon Shuttle leaves Bright Angel Lodge at 1:30 PM and arrives at the North Rim's Grand Canyon Lodge about 6:30 PM. The return trip leaves the North Rim each morning at 7 AM, arriving at the South Rim at about noon. One-way fare is $70, round-trip $130. A 50% deposit is required two weeks in advance. Reservations are required.

Bus Information Greyhound Lines (☎928/774–4573 or 800/231–2222 ⊕www.greyhound.com).

Contacts Flagstaff Express Shuttle (☎928/225–2290 or 800/563–1980 ⊕www.flagstaf fexpress.com). **Open Road Tours** (☎928/226–8060 or 877/226–8060 ⊕www. openroadtours.com).**Trans Canyon Shuttle** (☎928/638–2820).

∎ BY CAR

Most of Arizona's scenic highlights are many miles apart, and a car is essential for touring the state. However, you won't really need one if you're planning to visit only the Grand Canyon's most popular area, the South Rim. Some people choose to fly to the Grand Canyon and then hike, catch a shuttle or taxi, or sign on for bus tours or mule rides.

If you're driving to Arizona from the east, or coming up from the southern part of the state, the best access to the Grand Canyon is from Flagstaff. You can take U.S. 180 northwest (81 mi) to Grand Canyon Village on the South Rim. Or, for a scenic route with stopping points along the canyon rim, drive north on U.S. 89 from Flagstaff, turn left at the junction of AZ 64 (52 mi north of Flagstaff), which merges with U.S. 180 at Valle, and proceed north and west for an additional 57 mi until you reach Grand Canyon Village on the South Rim.

If you're crossing Arizona on Interstate 40 from the west, your most direct route to the South Rim is on AZ 64 (U.S. 180), which runs north from Williams for 58 mi to Grand Canyon Village. For road and weather conditions, call 928/638–7888 (recording).

To visit the North Rim of the canyon, proceed north from Flagstaff on U.S. 89 to Bitter Springs. Then take U.S. 89A to the junction of AZ 67. Travel south on AZ 67 for approximately 40 mi to the North Rim, which is 210 mi from Flagstaff.

If you are driving to Grand Canyon West from Kingman, take Stockton Hill Road exit off of Interstate 40. Head north 42 mi to Pierce Ferry Road. Travel north for 7 mi to Diamond Bar Road and turn east. In 21 mi, Diamond Bar Road comes to a dead end at Grand Canyon West Airport.

GASOLINE
The only gas station inside the national park on the South Rim is at Desert View, and this station operates only from March 31 to September 30 depending on snowfall. Gas is available year-round near the South Entrance at Moqui Lodge (though the lodge itself is now closed), in Tusayan, and at Cameron, to the east.

At the South Rim, in Grand Canyon Village, the Public Garage is a fully equipped AAA garage that provides auto repair daily 8 to noon and 1 to 5 as well as 24-hour emergency service. This is a garage for repairs only and does not sell gasoline.

At the North Rim, the Chevron service station, which repairs autos, is inside the park on the access road leading to the North Rim Campground. The station is open daily 7 to 7, mid-May through mid-October. No diesel fuel is available at the North Rim.

ROAD CONDITIONS
When driving off major highways in low-lying areas, watch for rain clouds. Flash floods from sudden summer rains can be deadly.

The South Rim stays open to auto traffic year-round, although access to Hermits Rest is limited to shuttle buses in summer because of congestion. Roads leading to the South Rim near Grand Canyon Village and the parking areas along the rim are congested in summer as well. If you visit from October through April, you can experience only light to moderate traffic and have no problem with parking.

Reaching elevations of 8,000 feet, the more remote North Rim has no services available from late October through mid-May. AZ 67 south of Jacob Lake is closed by the first heavy snowfall in November or December and remains closed until early to mid-May.

There are no services available at Grand Canyon West.

To check on Arizona road conditions, call the Arizona Department of Transportation's recorded hotline.

ROADSIDE EMERGENCIES
In the event of a roadside emergency, call 911. Depending on the location, either the state police or the county sheriff's department will respond. Call the city or village police department if you encounter trouble within the limits of a municipality. Indian reservations have tribal police headquarters, and rangers assist travelers within U.S. Forest Service boundaries.

Automobile Service Stations
Conoco (✉ Tusayan ☎928/638–2608).**Grand Canyon Garage** (✉ Grand Canyon Village ☎928/638–2631).**Jacob Lake Inn** (✉ Hwy.

67/U.S. 89A, Fredonia ☎928/643–
7232).

▌ BY TAXI

Visitors to the South Rim can
catch a cab from the Grand Canyon Airport and hotels in Tusayan by calling the taxi service
operated by Xanterra.

Contacts Xanterra South Rim
(☎928/638–2822).

▌ BY TRAIN

Amtrak offers train service from
stations nationwide to Flagstaff and Williams. To ride the
rails direct to the South Rim in
Grand Canyon National Park,
hop aboard the cozy cars on the
Grand Canyon Railway, which
has been taking spectators to the
Grand Canyon since 1901.

Information Amtrak (☎928/774–
8679 or 800/872–7245 ⊕www.
amtrak.com).**Grand Canyon Railway** (☎800/843–8724⊕www.
thetrain.com).

ON THE GROUND

▌ COMMUNICATIONS

INTERNET
Most hotels and motels in the region will offer some kind of high-speed Internet or Wi-Fi connection. You'll find Internet access at some of the park's hotels and motels; be sure to verify this in advance if it is important to you.

Contacts Cybercafes (⊕www. cybercafes.com) lists over 4,000 Internet cafés worldwide.

PUBLIC TELEPHONES
There are public telephones at all visitor centers and lodgings. Cell-phone reception is not possible in many areas of the park.

▌ EATING OUT
Except for the El Tovar Dining Room, food is pretty straightforward and simple fare at the Grand Canyon. The Bright Angel Lodge's Arizona Room offers steaks and other hearty meals. The cafeterias and fast-food spots offer filling, if uninspiring food.

RESERVATIONS & DRESS
Dress is never formal in a national park, but you may want to put on your best jeans if you intend to dine at the El Tovar Dining Room, the fanciest place in the park. Reservations are strongly recommend if you want to eat here during your stay; otherwise, they aren't accepted.

▌ EMERGENCIES
In case of a fire or medical emergency, dial 911; from in-park lodgings, dial 9-911. To report a security problem, contact the Park Police (☎ 928/638–7805), stationed at all visitor centers. There are no pharmacies at the North or South Rim. Prescriptions can be delivered daily to the South Rim Clinic from Flagstaff. A health center is staffed by physicians from 8 AM TO 6 PM, seven days a week (reduced hours in winter). Emergency medical services are available 24 hours a day.

Contacts Emergencies (☎911, 9–911 in park lodgings).**Grand Canyon Walk-in Clinic** (✉ Grand Canyon Village ☎928/638–2551). **North County Community Health Center** (✉ 1 Clinic Rd., Grand Canyon ☎928/638–2551).

▌ MONEY

BANKS
There is a full-service bank and ATM at the South Rim Chase Bank office in Market Plaza near the General Store and an ATM located at Maswik Lodge. Near the North Rim, there's an ATM at Jacob Lake Inn.

Contacts **Chase Bank** (☎928/638–2437).

CREDIT CARDS

Throughout this guide, the following abbreviations are used: **AE**, American Express; **D**, Discover; **DC**, Diners Club; **MC**, MasterCard; and **V**, Visa.

Reporting Lost Cards American Express (☎800/992–3404 ⊕www.americanexpress.com). **Diners Club** (☎800/234–6377 ⊕www.dinersclub.com). **Discover** (☎800/347–2683 ⊕www.discovercard.com). **MasterCard** (☎800/622–7747 ⊕www.mastercard.com). **Visa** (☎800/847–2911 ⊕www.visa.com).

TRAVELER'S CHECKS & CARDS

ATM machines in Arizona are ubiquitous, and it's the rare business that does not accept credit cards, so it's hard to think of a good reason to bother with traveler's checks. If you do plan on using them, ask before checking into a hotel room or sitting down to a meal to make sure the property accepts them, as not all Arizona businesses do.

PETS

Pets are allowed in Grand Canyon National Park; however, they must be on a leash at all times. Pets are not allowed below the rim or on park buses, with the exception of service animals. There's a kennel, near the Maswik Lodge, which houses cats and dogs. It's open daily from 7:30 AM to 5 PM. Reservations are highly recommended. No pets are allowed on the Hualapai Reservation at Grand Canyon West or on the Hualapai Reservation in Havasu Canyon.

Contacts **Grand Canyon Kennel** (☎928/638–0534).

▌POST OFFICE

On the South Rim, the Market Plaza shopping center near Yavapai Lodge has a post office that is open weekdays 9 to 4:30 and Saturday 11 to 1. On the North Rim, the post office is located in the Grand Canyon Lodge complex. It is open weekdays from 8 to noon and from 1 to 5.

For a unique postmark from the canyon floor, send a letter from Phantom Ranch or from Supai in Havasu Canyon—both make their way out of canyon by pack mule.

▌RESTROOMS

All visitor centers, lodgings, and restaurants have restrooms.

On the South Rim's Desert View Drive, there are restrooms at Desert View, Grandview Point, and the Tusayan Ruin and Museum. Restrooms on Hermit Road are at Hopi Point and at Hermits Rest. On the North Rim drives, there are restrooms at Point Imperial on Point Imperial Road and at Cape Royal on Cape Royal Road.

TAXES

Arizona state sales tax (called a transaction privilege tax), which applies to all purchases except food in grocery stores, is 5.6%. Flagstaff taxes purchases at a rate of 1.51%. When added to county taxes, the total sales tax in Flagstaff, to 7.91%. Total sales taxes throughout the state range from 7.3% to 10.1%. Sales taxes do not apply on Indian reservations.

TIME

Arizona is in the mountain time zone but Nevada, next door, is in the Pacific time zone. Arizona does not use daylight saving time, though, and as a result, from spring through fall, Nevada and Arizona observe the same hours. The Navajo Nation does observe daylight saving time, however, so it's always the same time on Navajo territory as in mountain time zone areas outside Arizona.

VISITOR INFORMATION

Every person arriving at the South or North Rim is given a detailed map of the area. Centers at both rims also publish a free newspaper, The Guide, which contains a detailed area map; it's available at the visitor center, entrance stations, and many of the lodging facilities and stores. The park also distributes Accessibility Guide, a free newsletter that details the facilities accessible to travelers with disabilities. Grand Canyon National Park is the contact for general information. Write ahead for a complimentary Trip Planner, updated regularly by the National Park Service.

Several Web sites are useful for trip-planning information, including the National Park Service's Web site, which has information on fees and permits. Try thecanyon.com, a commercial site where you'll find information on lodging, dining, and general park information. You can use the Xanterra Parks & Resorts Grand Canyon Web site to make reservations for park lodging, mule rides, bus tours, and some smooth-water rafting trips. The park service allows camping reservations to be made online as well, through the campground reservation vendor.

In summer, transportation-services desks are maintained at El Tovar, Bright Angel, Maswik Lodge, and Yavapai Lodge in Grand Canyon Village; in winter, the one at Yavapai is closed. The desks provide information and handle bookings, sightseeing tours, taxi and bus services, mule and horseback rides, and accommodations at Phantom Ranch (at the bottom of the Grand Canyon). The concierge at El Tovar can also arrange most tours, with the exception of mule rides and lodging at Phantom Ranch.

Grand Canyon Lodge has general information about local services available in summer when the North Rim is open.

The Williams and Forest Service Visitor Center, run by the U.S. Forest Service and the Williams Chamber of Commerce, offers information on the Kaibab National Forest and the entire Grand Canyon region.

Contacts Grand Canyon Chamber of Commerce (☎*928/638–2901* ⊕*www.grandcanyonchamber. com*).**Grand Canyon National Park** (☎*928/638–7888 recorded message* ⊕ *www.nps.gov/grca*). **Grand Canyon National Park Lodges** (☎*303/297–2757* ⊕ *www.grandcanyonlodges.com*). **Grand Canyon West** (✉ *Hualapai Reservation* ☎*702/878–9378 or 877/716–9378* ⊕ *www. destinationgrandcanyon.com*). **Havasupai Tourist Enterprise** (✉ *Supai* ☎*928/448–2141*⊕ *www. havasupaitribe.com*).**Kaibab National Forest, Tusayan Ranger District** (✉ *Hwy. 64, Tusayan* ☎*928/638–2443* ⊕ *www.fs.fed. us/r3/kai*).**Kaibab National Forest, Williams Ranger District** (✉ *742 S. Clover Rd., Williams* ☎*928/635–5600*⊕ *www.fs.fed. us/r3/kai*).**Kaibab Visitor Center** (✉ *Hwy 89A/AZ 67, Jacob Lake* ☎*928/643–7298*⊕ *www. fs.fed.us/r3/kai*).**Navajo Nation Tourism Dept. (Tuba City)** (✉ *Tuba City* ☎*928/871–6436*⊕ *www. discovernavajo.com*).**Williams Visitor Center** (✉ *200 W. Railroad Ave., at Grand Canyon Blvd., Williams* ☎*928/635– 1418 or 800/863–0546*⊕ *www. williamschamber.com*).

INDEX

NOTES

NOTES

NOTES

NOTES

NOTES

ABOUT OUR WRITERS

Over the last two decades, **Carrie Miner Frasure** has explored the vast reaches of Arizona from the low Sonoran Desert to high alpine forests. Since first encountering the Grand Canyon on the South Rim as a young girl in 1983, she has hiked miles of inner canyon trails, rafted the length of the Colorado River through the canyon, and extensively explored the rims and surrounding wilderness areas. While researching this book, Carrie revisited the Grand Canyon with her husband Billy—a first-timer to the sublime spectacle. They walked North and South Rim trails, explored the diverse countryside, wandered through historic buildings, meandered down scenic drives, and visited with Native American residents at the West Rim. Although Billy enjoyed the entire trip, his favorite experience was the view from the Skywalk, where a member of the Hualapai tribe pointed out the hidden figures of a thunderbird and a woman's profile embedded in the canyon walls. The primary writer for this guidebook, Carrie has published hundreds of articles and several books on the Southwest. She currently splits her time between the Sonoran Desert and the Arctic Circle, where she lives with husband and two sons.

Cara LaBrie is a Phoenix native who recently returned to Arizona after an eight-year absence. She has worked for years as a reporter and editor for newspapers across the country, including the Arizona Republic. Although she missed the stunning Arizona sunsets she says she didn't really appreciate the beauty of the desert until she returned. And as far as Cara is concerned, salsa isn't a condiment; it's a beverage. Cara updated the coverage of some sections of North-Central Arizona, which were included in the "What's Nearby" chapter.